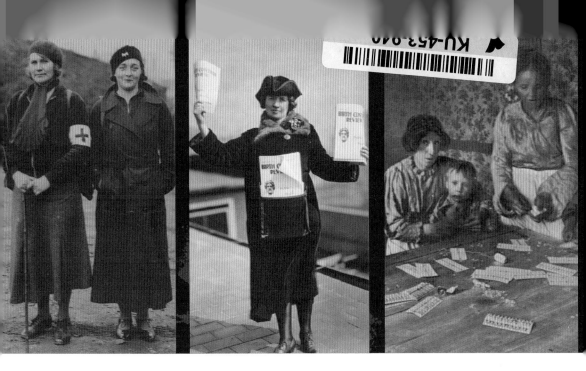

contents

Introduction

The Mary Quaile Club is pleased to present its fourth publication in which we highlight the role of women as activists; whether speaking, unionising, marching, protesting... or singing. The common theme to the articles is women challenging power and oppression.

This follows on from our three previous publications: *Northern ReSisters: Conversations with Radical Women, Dare to Be Free*, and *"For the sake of the women who are to come after,"* Manchester's *Radical Women 1914 to 1945.*

The Mary Quaile Club was set up in December 2013 with the aim of holding regular discussions on working class history and the links with contemporary political issues facing working people today. We take our name from Mary Quaile (1886 to 1958), an Irish migrant to Manchester. She rose from a Manchester café waitress to become one of the most well-known women trade unionists in Britain. Mary was an organiser for the Manchester and Salford Women's Trades Council and then took a post as the first national women's officer for TGWU. She also served on the TUC General Council for several years, and led a TUC women's trade union women's delegation to the Soviet Union for four months in 1925.

Over the past decade we have held numerous events; commissioned a play about Mary Quaile, *Dare to Be Free*; and set up a website on which we placed the complete minutes of the Manchester and Salford Women's Trades Council, which Bernadette Hyland transcribed from the hand-written original volumes. This can be found at www.mswtuc.co.uk.

Our contributors:

Naomi Bridges is a feminist, activist and professional irritant. Producer and podcaster, women's rights are her main focus.

Georgina Gittins started to research local history after she retired from mental health nursing, in particular the untold stories of people whose work has benefitted us all but who are unacknowledged and often unknown. She lived in Wrexham all of her life; if she is not researching, she is usually out walking with her son or feeding the cat.

Michael Herbert is a socialist historian. His published work includes *"Up Then Brave Women"*; Manchester Radical Women 1819-1918, *"For the Sake of the Women who are to come after"*: Manchester's Radical Women 1914-1945 and *Doctor Who and the Communist: Malcolm Hulke and his career in television.*

Bernadette Hyland is a writer and lifelong activist in her community and her trade union. Her writing reflects her grassroots politics and her disdain for the shallowness of present day society and its celebrity culture.

Katy Worley is a DJ turned activist, She became concerned about the erosion of women's rights brought about by gender identity ideology since 2017. She blogs, podcasts and organises events.

This publication has been sponsored by Unite the Union, Unite North East Region and NEU North East.

We would like to thank the Working Class Movement Library, Chetham's Library and Co-operative Archive for their assistance with the research for this publication.

Finally we would like to thank our designer, Mike Carter.

"...what is life without hope?": Sarah Parker Remond: a Black American Abolitionist in Britain

by Michael Herbert

Sarah was an American free black woman who came to Britain in 1858 to speak against slavery. She was born on 6th June 1826 in Salem, Massachusetts, the second youngest child of the ten offspring of two free black people, John and Nancy Remond, who married in the African Baptist Church in Boston in 1807.

Sarah says that Salem contained "about 25,000 inhabitants, who are characterised by general intelligence, industry and enterprise and few towns in the States can boast of more wealth and refinement than Salem." Her father had come to the United States, from Curacao, aged 10, in 1798 and ran a successful catering business, while her mother was born in Newton, seven miles from Boston, and was an accomplished cake-maker. Sarah says of her mother:

Nancy Remond is a woman possessing every characteristic. We were all trained to habits of industry, with a thorough knowledge of those domestic duties which particularly mark the genuine New England woman. With no private means, it was also most necessary. We were taught to knit and sew, and to cook every article of food placed upon the table. The most trifling affair was obliged to be well done. Her aim seemed to be to guard, and at the same time strengthen, her children, not only for the trials and

duties of life, but also to enable them to meet the terrible pressures which prejudice against color would force upon them. Our home discipline was what we needed, but it did not – could not, fit us for the scorn and contempt which met us on every hand when face to face with the world, where we met a community who hated all who were identified with an enslaved race. While our mother never excused those who unjustly persecuted those whose only crime was a dark complexion, her discipline taught us to gather strength from our own souls; and we felt the full force of the fact, that to be black was no crime, but an accident of birth.[1]

Sarah took great pleasure in reading:
...as we had no library, I read every book which came in my way, and, like Oliver Twist, I longed for more. Again and again mother would endeavour to have us placed in some private school, but being colored we were refused. We soon knew the real reason and the most bitter and indignant feelings were cherished by me against those who deprive me of the opportunity of gaining knowledge. My eldest brother had been admitted to one of the public schools, and at a much later period the three youngest children, including myself, were admitted to one of the public primary schools...Both teachers

1

always treated us with kindness. We had been in this school a very short time, when we were informed that the school committee contemplated founding a school exclusively for colored children.[2]

Despite the protests of their parents who did not want them to attend a school just for black children, the Remonds were asked to leave their school. The memory of this humiliation stayed with Sarah:
Separate churches and schools for colored persons are an immense disadvantage to the descendants of the African race, and a great drawback to their elevation. They are based completely on prejudice against color, the legitimate offspring of American slavery, and it is to be regretted that many well-wishers to the colored race assist in sustaining them. I never knew a pro-slavery man or woman who did not do all they could to encourage and keep up separate schools and churches, enforcing at the same time the idea that God intended such distinction to be made. There is a refinement of cruelty in the treatment of this class of persons rather difficult to describe to those who have never seen the working of prejudice against color. The more intelligence and refinement they possess, the more liable they are to insult. The chivalry of America seems to take immense satisfaction in insulting those who will feel it the most keenly.[3]

The family moved to Newport, Rhode Island, but Sarah and her brothers and sisters were still refused admittance to public schools. Eventually she received some education at a private school set up by a number of the black residents of the town. The family returned to Salem, where Sarah continued her education at home from books and from visitors to their house:
Although I had few leisure hours, I read more or less daily. Our home was constantly supplied with the best daily and weekly newspapers, and I could obtain from public libraries and often from the private libraries of friends, some of the best English and American literature. These were resources of which *even* prejudice could not deprive me. A book once obtained, I could peruse it with pleasure and profit... When some abolitionist who had buried all prejudice against color which education and habit had taught...when such a one was the guest of my parents, I treasured up in the storehouse of memory the information derived from conversations in the society of some of the most gifted of the sons and daughters of America...These opportunities were not frequent, but they were valuable. Reading was the staple and never–failing resource.[4]

Massachusetts was the birthplace of the Abolitionist movement. In 1831 Willam Lloyd Garrison began publishing *The Liberator,* which called for the immediate abolition of slavery, which was a minority view, even in the non-slave-owning states of the North. In the first issue, dated 1st January 1831, he stated his views on slavery very plainly:"I do not wish to think, or speak, or write, with moderation... I am in earnest — I will not equivocate — I will not excuse — I will not retreat a single inch — AND I WILL BE HEARD." The newspaper ran for 35 years, ceasing only after the end of the Civil War and the final abolition of slavery through tan Amendment to the Constitution at the end of 1865.

In the columns of *The Liberator* Garrison attacked both slave-owners and those who held that slavery could be abolished gradually. "If those who deserve the lash feel it and wince at it I shall be assured that I am striking the right persons in the right place." In 1832 he founded the New England Anti-Slavery Society; the following year he helped establish the American Anti-Slavery Society, writing its Declaration of Sentiments, and serving as its first corresponding secretary. Garrison also insisted that women should be admitted as members, and they became the backbone of the Abolitionist movement in organisations such as the Boston Female Anti-Slavery Society, whose membership includedNancy and her daughters.

Even in the slave-free northern states many of the population profited from slavery, directly or indirectly, and were as opposed to its abolition as Southerners. Consequently the Abolitionists were frequently subject to attacks, both verbal and physical: Garrison himself was assaulted by a pro-slavery mob in Boston in October 1835, narrowly escaping with his life. In November 1837 Elijah Lovejoy, an anti-slavery Minister and publisher, was shot dead during a mob attack in Alton, Illinois.

Sarah says of Garrison that her mother:
...hailed the advent of this young noble apostle of liberty with enthusiasm and among my earliest impressions is mingled the name of that now venerated friend of the oppressed, William L. Garrison. As years rolled on, I became more and more interested in every effort made in behalf of the enslaved ; the germ of a glorious reform was now planted, and had taken root ;

the American Anti-Slavery Society was founded, based upon principles which in every age had broken the bonds of the oppressor.[5]

From an early age Sarah was taken to Abolitionist meetings:

As time rolled on, the antagonism between freedom and slavery became more conflicting. I was led to investigate, to the best of my ability, the causes from which sprang such conflicting principles. At the same time, convinced that the anti-slavery element was the only source of hope for the slave, I also endeavoured to acquaint myself with the operations of the friends of freedom, whose principles will finally emancipate the bondmen.[6]

Her brother Charles Lennox Remond, born 1810, became an agent of the Massachusetts Anti-Slavery Society in 1838, speaking at many public meetings. In June 1840 he travelled with William Lloyd Garrison to the World Anti-Slavery Conventionin London, his fare paid for by female anti-slavery societies. Instead of returning immediately to the United States, Charles remained in Britain for a further 18 months, giving lectures in many parts of the country on slavery and abolition.

Sarah had personal experience of racism. On 4th May 1853 she and her sister Caroline Remond Putnam, who owned a number of hairdressing salons in Salem, went to see a performance of Donizetti's opera *Don Pasquale* at the Howard Athenaeum in Boston. On arrival they were told that as they were black they could not sit in the box they had paid for, only in the gallery. As they insisted on going to the box, the police were called and two officers forcibly ejected them from the building, resulting in Sarah suffering some injuries. She sued the theatre and won $500 in compensation; her action ended segregated seating at the hall.[7]

In 1857 Sarah in her turn also became an anti-slavery lecturer, embarking on her first tour around New York state with her brother Charles. Thereafter she found herself speaking every week. Towards the end of 1858 Sarah was invited to speak in Great Britain, arriving in January 1859 in Liverpool. Even before she landed, her name would have been known by anti-slavery activists in Great Britain. The *Anti-Slavery Advocate*, a newspaper founded in 1853, carried the following report in November 1858:

The following letter has just been received by a friend of ours from Miss Sarah P. Remond, a colored lady, a zealous and able anti-slavery

Charles Lenox Remond

lecturer, and sister to Mr. Charles L. Remond, who was well known in England in 1840 and 1841, an eloquent pleader on behalf of his oppressed race. As it appears that Miss Remond may shortly be expected amongst us, we publish her letter in order that it may serve in some degree as introduction to one who, from all we have ever heard of her, is entitled to our confidence, kindness, and respect:

Salem (Mass.) Sept. 18,1858.

Dear Friend, Your letter dated August 18th, was received. It reached my home while I was absent attending anti-slavery convention at Cape Cod, in the town of Harwich, in company with Parker Pillsbury, Mr. Foss, and my brother. Our meetings, eight in number, were well attended. On Sunday, although we had a large hall, many were obliged to go away unable to obtain entrance. I never looked upon a more closely packed audience. We endeavoured to speak the words of truth to them, and I am sure the meeting was a very successful one. I received last week a short but pleasant call from Mr. Garrison and an English gentleman, Mr. Robson, who has been travelling in America.

3

Mr. Robson seems to understand the character of our nation and the spirit of slavery. He is bearing very faithful testimony against the great crime of our age. There is a very strong effort being made at this time on the part of slaveholders and their allies to legalize the slave trade. Only think of it, in the nineteenth century, a nation which years ago declared the slave trade piracy, and at this time is making greater professions in favour of liberty and Christianity than any other nation in the world, endeavouring to legalize the traffic in the bodies and souls of men and women who are made but little lower than the angels.." Is it not enough to make one's heart sick

Oh God ! my every heart-string cries,
Dost Thou these scenes behold
In this our boasted Christian land,
And must the truth be told ?

It is true the traffic in slaves has always been carried on under our flag, but now there will be an attempt made to throw around this infamous crime the sanction of law. And why not I may ask, when the Supreme Court of the United States has declared that men and women with a dark complexion "have no rights which white men are bound to respect.' When I began to write to you I did not intend to write so much about the cause I feel so much interest in, but you know out of the abundance of the heart the mouth speaketh."

It gave me great satisfaction to hear of your safe arrival at Liverpool. To ride upon the waves of the ocean three thousand miles is really an event. I was exceedingly anxious to join you in your voyage; more so than I expressed in my letters to you. Feeling that you had no prejudice against color, I knew I should be sure of one person to speak a word with now and then. I still hope to reach London before winter, but I dread starting for many reasons. I do not fear the wind nor the waves, but I know that, matter how I go, the spirit of prejudice will meet me. I shall take passage from Boston in an English steamer.

You mention my brother's friends. It is a long time since he visited England, so I shall gather all my courage, and endeavour to depend upon myself. Parker Pillsbury will write to a friend of his to meet me at Liverpool, and I shall hope to get along very well. He wished me to remember him very kindly to you. He has visited me twice at my own home since I wrote to you last. I am very truly yours, Sarah Parker Remond.[8]

She gave her first lecture in Liverpool on 21st January 1859. The *Liverpool Mercury* in its report said that Sarah had expressed her "unbound indignation at the apathy which professing Christians throughout the whole of the United States professed" and ended with "an earnest appeal for the moral and religious sympathy and influence of free England in the abolition movement." Her voice was described as "clear and musical" and she displayed a "great flow of language."[9]

Over the next two years Sarah spoke at over forty meetings around the country as well as in Ireland. In October 1860 she wrote to Samuel May that "she had received the most hearty cooperation from genuine friends of our cause, in fact without their valuable aid in every direction, I could not have done the anti-slavery work I have."[10]

In June 1859, for instance, she spoke in the Music Hall, Store Street, Bedford Square, London:
She said she was the representative in the first place of four millions of human beings held in slavery in land boasting of its freedom — of 400,000 persons of colour nominally free, but treated worse than criminals. She was the representative also of that body of abolitionists in the United States, reproachfully called Garrissoians; an epithet, however, which she deemed it an honour to appropriate.

What was the crime of the millions thus enslaved ? The head and front of their offending was the colour of their skin. She did not represent the politics of the country, nor even the religious sentiment the country, for that had been corrupted by the influence of slavery. She pleaded especially on behalf of her own sex. Words were inadequate to express the depth of the infamy into which they were plunged by the cruelty and licentiousness of their brutal masters. If English women and English wives knew the unspeakable horrors to which their sex were exposed on southern plantations, they would freight every westward gale with the voice of their moral indignation, and demand for the black woman the protection and rights enjoyed the white.

It was dark and evil hour when the first slave-ship landed its unhallowed cargo on the soil of Virginia. But it was still darker one when the patriots of the revolution compromised their principles, and incorporated slavery in the federal constitution. There was this immeasurable difference between the condition

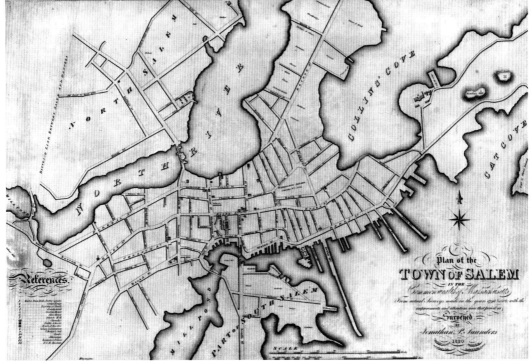

Map of Salem, Massachusetts, in 1820

of the poorer English woman and that of the slave woman—that their persons were free and their progeny their own: while the slavewoman was the victim of the heartless lust of her master, and the children whom she bore were his property. The situation of the free coloured population was also one of deep degradation. They were expelled from railway cars and steamboats, and excluded, even in the house of God, from the privileges common to other worshippers.

Miss Remond then traced the career of Mr. Garrison from the year 1833 to the present time, and recounted in touching manner the perils to which he had been exposed, the sacrifices he had made, and the progress which had been affected his unwearied labours during the last quarter of century. She had listened with indignation a few nights before to the statement that the slaves were happy and contented. If so, why had more than 40,000 fled to the free soil of Canada, and were ready to sell their lives in defence of the sovereignty of Queen Victoria?

The lecturer read an affecting account of the sale by auction of woman who was recommended on account of her being undistinguishable by complexion from the white race, for her unsullied virtue, her personal beauty, and her elevated piety, and who, for

these reasons, brought a high price that she might become the mistress of some depraved monster.

The lecturer paid a high tribute to Mr. Wendell Philipps, who with Mr. Garrison, had been traduced by the person whose assertions she already noticed, and concluded by pointing out the value to the American anti-slavery cause of those expressions of sympathy which it was in the power of the people England to send across the Atlantic, which would cheer the hearts of those engaged in the great struggle now going on. and tend greatly to advance the cause of negro emancipation. [11]

In September 1859 Sarah spoke at a meeting in Manchester, presided over by the Mayor of the city:

She said that she appeared as the agent of no society, speaking simply on her own responsibility, of her own knowledge and experience: but that in feeling and in principle she was identified with the Ultra-abolitionists of America.

Although the anti-slavery enterprise was begun some thirty years ago, the evil is still rampant in the land. As there are some young people present-and I am glad to see them here, for it is important that they should understand this subject - I shall briefly explain that there are

Family of slaves in Georgia, circa 1850

thirty two states, sixteen of which are free and sixteen slave states. The free states are in the north. The political feelings in the north and south are essentially different, so is the social life. In the north, democracy, not what the Americans call democracy, but the true principle of equal rights, prevails- I speak of the white population, mind-wealth is abundant; the country, in every material sense, flourishes. In the south, aristocratic feeling prevails, labour is dishonourable, five millions of poor whites live in the most degrading ignorance and destitution. I might dwell long on the miserable condition of these poor whites, the indirect victims of slavery; but I must go on to speak of the four millions of slaves. The slaves are essentially things, with no rights, political, social, domestic, or religious; the absolute victims of all but irresponsible power. For the slave there is no home, no love, no hope, no help; and what is life without hope? No writer can describe the slave's life; it cannot be told: the fullest description ever given to the world does but skim over the surface of this subject."[12]

In December 1859 Sarah spoke at the annual meeting of Leeds Young Men's Anti-Slavery Society alongside Frederick Douglass, a former slave, who had escaped to the North and become the most well-known black American in the United States for his vocal opposition to slavery. Douglass defended the action of John Brown, a white man who had led an armed raid on Harper's Ferry, Virginia, in October 1859 in an attempt to start a slave rebellion and who had been executed after it failed. The meeting was chaired by Edward Baines, the former editor of

the *Leeds Mercury*, who was now an MP.[13]

Some of her fellow Americans in Britain were less welcoming. In December 1859 Sarah went to the United States Embassy to get a visa for France but was turned away on the grounds that she was a "person of colour." After some publicity in the press, the visa was granted.

Somehow Sarah foundtime in her very busy schedule to attend classes between 1859 and 1861 at the Bedford College for Ladies in London, where she studied elocution, vocal music, ancient history, Latin, French, arithmetic, geography and English literature.

The election of Abraham Lincoln as President for the Republican Party in November 1860 lead to eleven states seceding from the Union in the first months of 1861 who formed the Confederate States of America, pledged to defend slavery at all costs. The Union refused to recognise the secession and hostilities broke out in April when the South attacked and captured the federal Fort Sumter in South Carolina. Both sides raised armies and fought bitterly and ferociously for four years with huge casualties and enormous devastation of land and property. The South won some initial victories, but eventually the larger population of the North and its industrial and economic strength told and General Robert E Lee surrendered the last Confederate army in April 1865.

Britain declared itself neutral in the conflict, although in November 1861, after a Union navy vessel stopped a British packet ship RMS *Trent* and removed two Confederate envoys - James Murray Mason and John Slidell - who were on their way to

Britain to press for recognition of the CSA, it seemed that there might be a war between the two countries over the issue. However Abraham Lincoln had the sense to disavow the action and to release the two men who continued on their journey to Britain.

The North blockaded Southern ports leading to what became known as the "Cotton Famine" when starved of the raw material from the South, much of the Lancashire cotton industry shut down by the end of 1861, throwing tens of thousands out of work. To avert starvation a relief committee was set up in Manchester. On 21st November 1862 *The Times* published a list of donations to the Lancashire and Cheshire Operatives Relief Fund which filled a page and included a £1 donation from Sarah.

Despite the hardships they were enduring many working people supported the North because they saw it as a war to end slavery. On 16th November 1863, for instance, Ernest Jones, a barrister and former leading Chartist, gave a lengthy speech entitled "Ihe Slaveholder's War" in Ashton-under-Lyne Town Hall, which he ended by stating:
Those base planters did not know what English working men were made of. They deemed we should never enquire about the justness of their cause, but that cotton was our God, and we should obey his mandates. Therefore, they sent their agents over to us, appealing to our lowest instincts—to our most sordid self-interests. But woe to a people that puts its interests before its duties. It will find, when the day of reckoning comes, that its real interests and duties are identical, and that it sacrificed the one when it deserted the other. But you have not done so. You have said, "Shew me who is in the right, and I will tell you who is my friend"—and you will meet your reward—for the key that shall re-open our closed factories is the sword of the victorious North. By your conduct in this time of trial, you have laid one more laurel on the time honoured brows of our county.[14]

Against this sentiment Confederacy propagandists in Britain devoted a great deal of time and money in an effort to win over public opinion in support of the South, portraying it as a struggle for freedom, and trying to capitalise upon the economic distress in the north of England. Liverpool businessmen James Spence, who had written a book *The American Union* supporting the South, published in September 1861, offered his services to the CSA and was very active in Lancashire where he recruited two former Chartists - William Aitken and Mortimer Grimshaw – to organise meetings in an effort to win over the

Frederick Douglass

cotton workers to the South's cause.[15]

Once the Civil War began, Sarah worked to build support in Britain for the Union cause and was joined by her sister Caroline and her nephew Edmund, after her sister's husband had died.[16]

In September 1861 Sarah addressed the 5th Annual Meeting of the National Association for the Promotion of Social Science, which that year was held in Dublin. Unusually among Victorian societies the Association allowed women both to attend *and* present papers. Her paper, "American Slavery and its influence on Great Britain," was published the following year in the record of the meeting:
The influence of nation upon nation can scarcely be over-estimated since steam has brought the inhabitants of distant countries into more intimate relations with each other. No two countries separated by the same distance have been more closely connected through many channels than the States of North America and Great Britain, and the influence of national character becomes a matter of serious importance. Chattel slavery as it exists in the Southern States of North America is the colossal evil, the prolific source which has corrupted the public opinion throughout the Republic, North as well as South. By the laws of the slaveholding States four millions of men, women and children have no more rights than an ox or sheep. This complete annihilation of the manhood and

The 54th Massachusetts Infantry Regiment at the Second Battle of Fort Wagner, 18th July, 1863

womanhood of human beings is supported and sustained by the compromises of the constitution.

From 1620 until 1787 slavery had no legal protection except in the most limited sense. In 1788, when the constitution was drafted and the present government formed, the complete sacrifice of the African was the price which purchased that result, and certain provisions of the Federal Constitution pledged the States, North and South, to maintain slavery.

First, by allowing the continuation of the foreign Slave Trade until 1808, although after that date by law it was declared to be piracy; yet in reality it has never been discontinued, as slaves have from time to time been sent from Cuba into the slave states. Slavers have been fitted out from New Orleans, New York, Boston, and other American cities, and many Africans landed, direct from Africa, in Texas, Florida, and Louisiana; and negroes who cannot speak the English language are at work on the plantations of the South. Great Britain has spent forty millions, and is still willing to assist in suppressing the foreign slave trade. The American Government has been unwilling to make any effectual treaty to bring about this desirable result and Cuba imports annually about forty to fifty thousand slaves. When Lord John Russell stated that: "Spain was not the only power committed to the slave trade, and that the American flag covered it to a large extent, and that the absence of the right of search increased the difficulty of dealing with slaves on the open sea" his Lordship placed the Government of the United States in the true position which it occupies in this abominable traffic.

Secondly, by the three-fifth representation – allowing five slaves to count as three votes – thus giving additional power to the owners of slaves. Thirdly, by the Fugitive Slave Act. Fourthly, for the suppression of any insurrectionary movement on the part of the slave population.

These four important provisions in the constitution reveal the basis on which the slave system rests; and although many other causes have given new vitality to the evil, the constitutional provisions have been, and still are, the Gibraltar of the slaveholders and their northern allies. The infamous Fugitive Slave Law of 1850, which denies its wretched victims trial

Black soldier in Union army uniform with family

by jury, and under which many free persons of colour have been doomed to a life of slavery, declares, Section 7, "Any person obstructing the arrest of a fugitive, or attempting his or her escape, or harbouring and concealing a fugitive knowing him to be such, shall be subject to a fine not exceeding one thousand dollars, and to be imprisoned not exceeding six months; and shall also forfeit and pay the sum of one thousand dollars for each fugitive lost." This is only one of the provisions of a law which is disgrace to civilisation.

Then followed the Dred Scott decision declaring that "black men and women have no rights which white men are bound to respect." The evil principle, embedded in the constitution at that early period of the history of nation, has resulted in a series of evil and unjust laws, which fall with overwhelming weight upon the oppressed African and his descendants, which have perverted the moral vision of the American people.

This corrupt public opinion operates in many ways upon Great Britain, but most decidedly in the attempt to transplant to the dominions of Queen Victoria the pernicious prejudice against

the colour of the African, whether he be a slave or nominally free, which is one of the many sad results of slavery in the States. In some of the Canadian towns the children of some of Her Majesty's most loyal subjects, have been placed in separate schools, only because they have a dark complexion. In other instances they have been placed in a corner of the regular Government schools, and British subjects haven obliged to submit to these dignities. In other instances the children of the coloured citizens have been obliged to walk not infrequently a long distance to one of these separate Government schools, while the child of the white citizen could attend the school in the locality to which the coloured child by right should be allowed access. In one of the churches at Vancouver's Island separate pews have been provided for coloured persons, in imitation of the American custom, this insulting an already deeply-injured race. [17]

Back in Sarah's home state a black regiment, the 54th Regiment Massachusetts Volunteer Infantry, was formed in February 1863, with her brother Charles acting as a recruiting agent. The black soldiers fought very bravely in an uphill attack on a

Confederate fort in Charleston, South Carolina, on 18th July 1863, suffering many casualties. (The story of the regiment is depicted in a film called *Glory* (1989). In all some 180,000 black soldiers served in the Union army in the course of the war.

In 1864 the London Ladies Emancipation Society - an anti-slavery group, founded in August 1863 by Clementia Taylor - in which Sarah was actively involved as one of its Executive Committee - published a pamphlet *The Negroes and Anglo-Africans as Freedman and Soldiers*, which she had compiled from newspapers reports with her own commentary added:

A new era has at last dawned for the black race, and at the present time they occupy a conspicuous position and take an active part in the stirring events now going in the States. Whether we consider their position as nominally free, as freedman, or as soldiers, every friend of that deeply injured race will watch their progress with hope and the most intense interest. As freedman and as soldiers they have fulfilled the expectations of their most sanguine friends...[18]

In 1866 Sarah was one of 1499 women who signed the first petition calling for Votes for Women which was presented to the House of Commons by John Stuart Mill, MP, on 7th June of that year, marking the beginning of a decades-long suffrage campaign which only ended in 1928 when women finally obtained the right to vote on the same terms as men.

Sarah had been studying at the University College, London, to become a nurse and in 1866 she left Britain to study midwifery at the Hospital St. Maria Nuovo in Florence. The hospital's archives in Florence contain two letters of recommendation; one, from Sister Rosmonda praised her skills, attention and kindness toward her patients; the other from Dr Berkeley Hill, Head Surgeon ofCollege, who praised the constant close attention Sarah paid to the welfare of the patients. She graduated in 1868.[19]

Although living in Italy, Sarah remained in touch with events in the USA where for black Americans the long-awaited dream of emancipation quickly turned sour in the aftermath of the Civil War. The decade of Reconstruction after 1865 - which allowed the defeated Southern states to be readmitted into the Union - was often a cloak for organised and sustained violence against the black population in the South, who were denied the civil and political rights supposedly guaranteed by the 13th Amendment to the Constitution which had abolished slavery in December 1865. On 22nd September 1866 the *Daily News* in London printed a letter from her, sent from Florence, in which she eloquently outlined the situation:

Sir, -Will you allow me to say a word in reference to the reactionary movement against the coloured race in the United States? It seems almost like trifling to write a short letter upon a subject so important, and teeming with so many facts, to prove that a new leaf is now being turned over in the history of the negro, and that there is a reaction ; a most intense reaction, against that race in the United States Let no friend of justice ignore that fact. What is the principal cause of the political conflict now going on? Never has there been more at stake than the present position of affairs involves. Why does the conflict assume such gigantic proportions? Why is it that Reconstruction has become so exceedingly difficult. Why is that party spirit is now reaching a height almost, if not quite beyond, any political struggle known even in that country so accustomed to political conflicts? Why is that in so many of the neither the freedmen nor their friends find any longer suitable protection? Why is it that the only really liberal newspaper that was published at New Orleans is now discontinued? What was the cause of the riot at New Orleans? Why were the men who served the country in her hour of need shot like dogs?

There is but one answer, and one source from which from which all these difficulties emanate – slavery in the past and its hateful remnants in the present. The Southerners and their Northern allies are determined that the black race shall not be recognized, shall not receive justice. They are determined to prevent the consummation of emancipation, to make freedom almost nominal. Reconstruction cannot be permanently settled until hatred of the coloured race is kept in check or exterminated. No one who has kept pace with the history of the coloured race can hope to re-educate a nation at once: therefore the only remedy is to check this hatred; made up of fashion, prejudice and intense ignorance.

This is the prolific source of the struggle between the contending political parties. The combatants may or may not recognize this tact. It assumes many, many shapes, puts on and off at pleasure such a variety of costumes, adapts itself to almost all circumstances with so much skill, that at first only its victims can detect it.

Fresh hatred seems to have been added to the old stock, and then taken complete possession of the Southerners and their Northern allies. The same elements animated by the same spirit which produced the civil war, starved Northern prisoners, and then assassinated the President when he became the firm friend of the slave population, now desire to gain new political strength. The Southern chivalry now demand that all their former slave population shall be represented in Congress, instead of the three-fifths representation which they formerly possessed. What bold injustice! Deny a race their civil and political rights and then endeavour to use them as an element of political strength to degrade them. Should they obtain this, perhaps another generation would pass before the consummation of emancipation. Many Republicans are deserting their principles, and joining the ranks of the enemy. Who can foresee the result of the coming contest? It may be that another fiery trial awaits the tried but faithful friends of the Republic.

A share of the same feeling of hatred towards the coloured race can now be seen most clearly in the minds of many Englishmen, of whom Mr. Thomas Carlyle is the best representative. He has special claims to the gratitude of negro haters on both sides of the Atlantic. I know of no man who could so consistently be the defender of Mr. Byre and the Jamaica massacre as Mr. Carlyle. It seems to be a most congenial occupation. He does his work *con amore*. The name of Mr. Thomas Carlyle, the literary leader of public opinion, has been for many years synonymous with all that is ungenerous and wantonly insulting to the negro race. His position as a literary man has given him the power of influencing the minds of the young. The same influence has been for many years a weapon in the hands of our enemies for adding deeper and more scornful insults. Negro haters on both sides of the Atlantic have again and again repeated his offensive insults, and his outspoken hatred in his recent letter against a race because they chance to be of a darker hue than himself is a fit offering to the spirit which seeks to defend might against right. Why Mr. Carlyle considers it his duty to attack a defenceless race with such hatred and passionate fury is a problem which I leave his many admirers on both sides of the Atlantic to solve.[20]

Sarah got married to an Italian Lazzaro Pinto in 1877 but the marriage does not appear to have lasted long. She later moved to Rome where her sisters Caroline and Maritcha joined her. Frederick Douglass visited them in January 1887. Sarah wrote to him a few months later:

Piazza Barberina No. 6
Primo Piano
Roma
Italia

July 8th 1887

My dear friend Frederick Douglass.
I have just received the promised and welcome letter dated July the 2nd. You did not direct it right and therefore it has been detained till today, although the Postmen know where I am. I hope you will receive this before you sail for America. The above address will find me till I write you to the contrary. It will be useless for me to write to my friends as you will be no longer in England. I write to you by return of the Post, and shall hope to hear again from you just as soon as you are rested after your ocean voyage. Ill as I was from sea sickness, I can never forget the beauty, and at times the awful grandeur of the Atlantic ocean! Broad and deep as it is we will have a chat now and then on paper. Rome is now quite deserted so far as the birds of winter passage are concerned, every day since you left the English speaking people have been going out of Rome and the Italians some of them go to the sea, country, et cetera. Rome at this season is quite another place. No one knows Italy till they see it in summer. The beauty heightens with the heat. I do not like the heat, but it does me good.

The lovely Pincio is always beautiful and I often seek a shady nook even at the noon day hour when the fierce sun comes down with intense white heat there is always a cool spot to be found there. The summer months often cure invalids if they can be persuaded to try it, and lead the right kind of life. I have some interesting facts on this point. You know all of my kin took flight some time ago. Mrs. Edmund and her father leave in a few days I believe then I shall be obliged to speak mostly Italian as there will be perhaps in all Rome only two or three persons that I know who speak English. The Italian Parliament closed its session yesterday. The debates have been of unusual interest lately. Please give my kind regards to Mrs Douglass, and with my most cordial regards for yourself I

Sarah Parker Remond's memorial plaque, Rome

am always most sincerelyYoursSarah Remond Pintor.P.S. I hope you can read this. In summer we have to shut windows and blinds to keep out the heat and one has to add instinct to sight in all they do for many hours of the day as you probably know.[21]

Sarah died on 13th December 1894 and is buried in Rome. Her grave is now marked by a commemorative plaque.

References

[1] "A Coloured Lady Lecturer," *The English Woman's Journal*, June 1861, p 270.

[2] "A Coloured Lady Lecturer," *The English Woman's Journal*, June 1861,p. 270

[3] "A Coloured Lady Lecturer," *The English Woman's Journal*, June 1861,p. 272.

[4] "A Coloured Lady Lecturer," *The English Woman's Journal*, June 1861, pp. 272-3.

[5] "A Coloured Lady Lecturer," *The English Woman's Journal*, June 1861, pp. 273-274.

[6] "A Coloured Lecturer," *The English Woman's Journal*, June 1861, p.274.

[7] Dorothy Burnett Palmer, "The Remonds of Salem, Massachusetts: A Nineteenth Century Family Revisited," *Proceedings of the American Antiquarian Society*, (1986), p. 282-83.

[8] *Anti-Slavery Advocate*, 1st November 1858, pp, 3-4.

[9] Dorothy Burnett Palmer, "The Remonds of Salem, Massachusetts: A Nineteenth Century Family Revisited," *Proceedings of the American Antiquarian Society*, (1986), p. 285.

[10] Dorothy Burnett Palmer, "The Remonds of Salem, Massachusetts: A Nineteenth Century Family Revisited," *Proceedings of the American Antiquarian Society*, (1986), pp. 285-286.

[11] *Anti-Slavery Advocate*, 1st July 1859, p.7.

[12] *Manchester Weekly Times*, 17th September 1859, p.5.

[13] *Leeds Times*, 24th December 1859, p. 3.

[14] The speech was published by the Ashton-under-Lyne Emancipation Society https://minorvictorianwriters.org.uk/jones/c slaveholder%27s war.htm

[15] Amanda Foreman, *A World on Fire* (2010), pp. 272-3.

[16] https://streetsofsalem.com/2020/12/26/caroline-remond-putnam/

[17] *Transactions of the National Association for the Promotion of Social Science, 1861* (1862), pp. 688-691.

[18] Sarah Parker Remond, *The Negroes and Anglo-Africans as Freedman and Soldiers* (1864).

[19] Sirpa Salenius, "Short Takes: In the words of Sarah Parker Remond" https://www.ucl.ac.uk/racism-racialisation/transcript-words-sarah-parker-remond

[20] *Daily News*, 22nd September 1865. The New Orleans Massacre occurred on 30th July 1866 when a peaceful demonstration of mostly black Freemen was set upon by a mob of white rioters, many of whom had been soldiers in the Confederate army. The best estimates are that at least 40 black people were murdered and several hundred injured. Edward Eyre was Governor of Jamaica who in October 1865 brutally suppressed the Morant Bay Rebellion. Over 400 black people were murdered in the reprisals, some 600 flogged, and at least 1000 houses were burned down. Eyre's supporters in Britain included Thomas Carlyle and John Ruskin.

[21] Leigh Fought: "Sarah Remond Pintor in Rome, July 8, 1887, " http://leighfought.blogspot.com/2018/07/sarah-remond-pintor-in-rome-july-8-1887.html

Miss Nellie Kay: Organiser of the Manchester Tailoresses

by Bernadette Hyland

I first came across Miss Nellie Kay when I was transcribing the Minute Books of the Manchester and Salford Women's Trades Council (MSWTUC), formed on 1st February 1895 by local philanthropists including C.P. Scott, the editor of the *Manchester Guardian*. Women trade unionists were rare in the late C19th: few of them wrote an autobiography or even appear in trade union histories.

I was fascinated by who this woman was and how and why she became an organiser of tailoresses. Luckily I had the MSWTUC Minute Books and Annual Reports which catalogued her activity and led me to the journal of the Amalgamated Society of Tailors (AST).

Miss Kay was part of a growing trade union and socialist movement that would change, although slowly, the lives of working class women and men in industrial cities such as Manchester. I was also interested in her because of her possible Jewish identity and her radicalism. She was the pioneering first woman organiser of the tailoresses and it was the actions of Miss Kay and her sister tailoresses that changed the history of the AST by forcing it to accept women into their union and become the Amalgamated Society of Tailors *and* Tailoresses.

Working class women were lucky to have an organisation such as the MSWTUC. The Council did not just encourage and promote working women to set up unions but it also sought a broader role to bring about change in society. It exposed the harsh working and living lives of women workers and wanted legislation passed to obtain fair wages for women workers, shorter hours and safer places of work. The Council was an important women-led and organised grouping that would give women such as Nellie Kay a support group for her trade union activity.

The MSWTUC employed two Organising Secretaries who did the day-to-day work with the women workers. At this time, although many women worked, few of them were in trade unions. Men dominated trade unions and often saw women workers as a threat to their wages and conditions. Most of them did not want women in their workplace, never mind in their union.

The minutes of the Council reveal an organisation that worked hard at organising poor women workers in workplaces as diverse as tailoring, boxmaking, printing and in laundries. By 1900 it had 950 members and two paid organisers: Sarah Dickenson and Frances Ashwell (after 1900 Eva Gore Booth). The minutes show that on occasions women workers were quite prepared to walk out of workplaces where they were treated badly by

Hook and eye carding

A number of trade unions organised male craft workers in tailoring, including the Amalgamated Society of Tailors and Tailoresses, the Scottish Operative Tailors, Manchester Jewish Society, Leeds Jewish Society, the Clothiers' Operative Society, the United Garment Workers, the Army Clothing Employers, the Independent Tailors' Union, the Military and Uniform Tailors' Union.

Most of the women involved in the tailoring trade were not classed as craft workers. They had no formal training, instead learning the trade from their fathers, brothers and uncles, often through home working. The term "tailoring" covered a wide variety of skilled and unskilled work including shirtmakers, handkerchief hemmers, vest makers, trouser makers, jackets makers etc. The use of sewing machines by women was seen as a threat by the male tailors who saw themselves as craft workers and "knights of the needle".

employers; The Council then stepping in to support these women and encourage them to organise themselves collectively into unions.

Organising poorly paid women workers was not easy. The Annual Reports of the MSWTUC outlined the barriers felt by working class women and how they responded. In 1902 the Annual Report explained how they set up a Tea Fund to buy tea, sugar, milk and cake for women attending meetings after work: **It was found that the tea was a great convenience, as many of the women live in outlying districts, they are naturally anxious to hurry home to tea when their work is over and it is both inconvenient and expensive for them to come back to meetings in the evening. We are glad to say that the tea had good results in introducing a social element that promoted good fellowship and a friendly spirit among the members, and the attendance has largely increased.**[1]

In 1903 the Annual Report of the Council explained: "For however severely trade grievances may be felt, the first steps in organisation are always difficult. The timidity of inexperience is hard to overcome, and people naturally fear to jeopardise their week's earnings."[2]

Few women were recognised as skilled workers, and lacking craft training they were often used by employers to undermine the pay rates established by male workers. The tailoring trade in Manchester was an important industry in the city which included some of the poorest workers who were often migrants eg including Irish and Jewish women. The Census of 1901 showed that 237,185 people were employed in the trade across the country but that only some 40,000 were in trade unions.

The poorest women worked at home or in small workshops and backstreet factories. Of these married women with children - who were forced to work at home - were the worst paid. A survey in Manchester, published in 1913, noted how "home workers, with their entire lack of organisation....isolated from each other, and suffering from the results of the complete confusion that appears to prevail in these trades." This was contrasted with the cotton trade "where they form a compact organised body with the force of the men's unions behind them..."[3] But, as the numbers of women in the industry grew, eventually the tailoring unions decided to invite them to become members.

In December 1897 the MSWTUC minutes noted how an employer, Messrs. John Noble, had brought in lower paid Jewish workers (presumably women) which meant that *all* the workers saw a fall in their wages. The workers had contacted the Council and Mr. G.D. Kelly of the Manchester Trades and Labour Council who had organised a meeting to encourage the women to set up a trade union. Unfortunately the Minutes record that rhe workers "had since regained part of their lost prices, and had been successful in their attempt to secure the abolition of Jewish labour at the factory... Since then they had come to see that they required a trade union to protect their interests. They had applied to the M. S. & D. Women's Trade Union Council to help them to become organised".[4]

There is a tension here. Unorganised Jewish labour is seen as a threat by the other women workers, the Women's Trades Council and the male Manchester

Trades and Labour Council. The answer is seen as organising the women workers into a union, but not challenging the anti-semitism of both the employer and other workers.

In Manchester Jewish people lived alongside other poor immigrant communities. The inner city was divided between the Irish who lived in New Cross and Little Ireland, the Jews in the Strangeways and Redbank districts, and the Italians in the Ancoats area.

In the Amalgamated Society of Tailors the local officers had Irish names ie Kelley and Flynn. Miss Kay organised meetings at the Shamrock Hall which was in the Irish area on Rochdale Road. Unfortunately most of the Tailoresses remained anonymous; it is only by looking at the few photographs of women workers from this era that you can see Irish and Jewish faces staring intently at the camera.

The Manchester Jewish community was established in 1794 and was boosted in the 1840s by the influx of poor Jews from Eastern Europe. They were more orthodox, setting up their own places of worship, and working in a narrow range of trades. By 1891 the Chief Constable reported that there were 15,000-16,000 Jews in Manchester, of whom 70% were east European immigrants. As the community grew so did the proportion of east Europeans; by 1914 it was four fifths of the total population.[5]

Of this 30,000 a minority were active in trade unions, anarchist and socialist groups. In 1890 a strike by Jewish Machinists, Tailors and Pressers represented the first entry of Manchester Jewish workers into trade union activity and labour movement history. Jewish women would play their own separate role, which has often been excluded from this history.

As early as March 1898 Jewish women were getting organised into their own union: the Minutes of the Council recorded that "The Jewish Tailoresses' Union continued to prosper & the membership has now increased to over 100."[6]

In September 1898 the Council was asked by the Jewish Machiner's, Tailors' and Pressers' Union to help support the Jewish Tailoresses' Union which had dwindled down to just 25 members. The Organising Secretaries, Mrs Dickenson and Miss Ashwell, visited the girls at work, but as the girls only spoke Yiddish and German they had great difficulty communicating with them. The girls had asked that literature be provided explaining trade unionism but this had not been done by the union. Mrs Dickenson and Miss Ashwell had started attending the weekly meetings of the Tailoresses' Union.[7]

The catalyst for organising tailoresses into the main union - the Amalgamated Society of Tailors- was a strike by male tailors in Oldham in 1899. They objected to the Co-operative Wholesale Society (CWS) paying 50% less for making garments than the recognised rate in Lancashire. The Society was paying female labour (who did two-thirds of the work) at a lower rate and was also sending out work to "sweating dens".

The Oldham strike enraged both the male and female workers – both union and non union members -at the factory in Broughton, Salford when the CWS tried to move the work of the men from Oldham to its Broughton factory. Together they went on strike.

The trade journal *Tailor and Cutter* reported:
There are now on strike 33 members of the Amalgamated Society of Tailors, 30 clothiers' operatives, 400 women workers, and about a 100 Jews consisting chiefly of those who have ceased to work for middlemen to whom the Wholesale Society was sending strike trade.   In addition to the immediate cause of the strike the workpeople have numerous other grievances against the Co-operative Wholesale Society, and they have presented to the directors a statement of their case in which they ask that owing to the irregular manner in which they have been employed during the busy season, there shall, during slack seasons, be a fair and equitable division of the trade amongst the persons employed in the different sections of the departments; also that reasonable limits be placed on the number of hours worked as overtime and thus it be deemed unnecessary for piece workers to remain in the factory at times when it is not possible to give them employment, and that no employee shall be dismissed without any reason being given.[8]

The *Manchester Evening News* reported on 30th June 1899 that the AST had made a financial appeal on behalf of the Tailoresses for £200 per week which was needed as many of the women were widows who had families to support. The following month it reported on how the Broughton women workers went up to Oldham to support the strike and to encourage the Tailoresses at the factory to walk out:
About seven or eight waggonette and omnibus

loads of tailors and tailoresses, who are on strike at the Co-operative Wholesale Society's workshop in Manchester, visited Oldham on Saturday. They might easily have been mistaken—so smartly got-up were most of the girls—for a Sunday school picnic but for the placards on the vehicles, which notified to the public that the occupants were strike hands, and appealed for assistance in a struggle against inhumanity. After the visitors had been driven round the town an open-air meeting was held near the Park, but there were very few listeners beyond the demonstrators themselves. A number of speeches were delivered, and a resolution was adopted calling the tailoresses of the Oldham Co-operative societies to strike work.[9]

The Amalgamated Society of Tailors recognised that they had to recruit tailoresses into their union in order to stop the women being used to undermine strikes such as at Oldham. The Annual Report of the MSWTUC for 1900 recorded that "the Tailoresses section was founded in 1899 and officials of Amalgamated Tailors' Society agreed to temporary take charge of the women's interests and to conduct their business for them. It was felt at the end of the first year the time had come for the tailoresses should manage their own affairs."[10.]

Thus In December 1900 a general meeting of the society was called at which a separate branch for tailoresses was established. Miss Chadwick was elected President, Miss Kay was elected Secretary and a committee of women was set up.[11]

This is where Miss Nellie Kay enters the story. But who is she? I am assuming she was Jewish. In an interview she gave to the Journal of ASTT in 1902 she said came from a family of tailors and had been working since the age of 16 in the trade. "My family have been tailors for generations, so I ought to know something about the trade.".[12]

However she cannot be found in the census of 1901 or 1911. Perhaps "Kay" was not her name at birth, Jewish migrants often anglicised their names on arriving in Britain.

In her comments about the Tailoresses' branch she dates its beginnings to the Oldham strike. "We only began about two and a half years ago, and we have about 100 members. In the city and district there are about 50 workshops - great and small - and we estimate the number of women and girl-workers in the tailoring trade between 4,000 and 5,000.[13]

It seems highly likely that she was one of the women at the Broughton branch of the CWS who went out on strike with the tailors. They were the largest employers at the time as she comments: "Oh, the Co-operative Wholesale Society employ by far the largest number of women and girls. I dare say in the busy season nearly 500 are engaged there."

But, according to Miss Kay, the CWS were not model employers:

I am sorry to say we have had a lot of trouble with them. Indeed, the birth of our women's branch dates from the time of the struggle between the Oldham Co-operative Society and its tailors - a struggle which extended to the C.W.S. Owing to some dispute at Oldham, the Society sent their work to Manchester to be completed. The tailors at the C.W.S. objected to doing work about which their brother "knights of the needle" of another town were disputing, and they came out on strike. The women came out with them. That is two and a half years ago.[14]

The Broughton factory was built in 1897 and was seen as a flagship for the CWS and the tailoring trade. In July 1899 the *Oldham Wheatsheaf*, a monthly Co-operative journal, reported on the new building and its workers. Some 500 people worked there, of which 200 were women.

Doing a superior class of work the management are able to pay a better wage and thus they have the opportunity to select a superior class of workpeople thus ensuring first class work with many other advantages to worker, employer and customer alike..."We would not fail to observe that the class of girls employed is superior to those we see coming away from some of the clothing factories here in Manchester.[15]

Ironically it is this group of women that decide to walk out with the male trade unionists, rather than do the work of the Oldham tailors. Perhaps a number of these women were already members of the Jewish Tailoresses' Union or active in the radical and socialist organisations which some Jewish and Irish people were now joining.

Unfortunately the women in the Oldham Factory did not join the male tailors on strike. Indeed the *Oldham Industries Coop Society Record* of June 1899 reported that the 36 female hands had signed a letter stating: "The females employed at the above from (Coop Store) of the tailoring department beg to say we are satisfied with the conditions of the management and price paid to us by the above firm."[16]

Workers in the Broughton CWS factory. Image courtesy of the Co-operative archive

Maybe the women were angry at the male tailors whom they felt wanted them thrown out of work. But the union said: "if a woman did the same work as a man she should be paid the same price, and further we admitted women as members of our union."[17]

After the strike was resolved and the workers at both factories went back to work the Tailoresses were brought into the AST and it became the ASTT. But trouble rumbled on as the management at the Broughton factory started victimising the Tailoresses.

In November 1900 the minutes of the MSWTUC recorded:
A report was given on the state of the Tailoresses' Society. The membership was decreasing considerably among the girls at the Co-operative Tailoring Factory at Lower Broughton. This was thought to be due to the action of the manager. He had treated the girls who belong to the union very unfairly making trivial excuses to get rid of them, and giving the best positions to the non-union girls. Before taking action the Council decided to collect some definite information from girls who had been discharged without any adequate reason. The Secretaries were instructed to get together some of the aggrieved girls to attend at the office on Monday night and meet members of the Council. A deputation was formed to wait on the directors of the Co-operative Society. The deputation to consist of Miss Bulley, Mr. Johnstone and the Secretaries.[18]

In December 1901 Miss Kay took up the role of organiser for the Manchester and Salford tailoresses who were unique in the country as organised women in a largely craft based male trade. The Council minutes noted: "She had already done a good deal of visiting and persuaded some new members to join. Miss Kay was now able to attend Council meetings, as she had given up her tailoring work.[19] It seems highly likely that she was part of the Jewish Tailoresses' Union, while the fact she has the confidence to start organising before she was appointed to the post organiser points to a woman who was not afraid to be outspoken at work – and was perhaps also active outside work in a radical organisation.

Miss Kay was immediately faced with an issue.

In September 1901 the CWS had reduced the amount paid to workers: they were losing 2s per week. Miss Kay stepped in and had an interview with the Co-operative directors on 3rd October about the reduction in prices. They stated that the reduction would not affect weekly earnings because there would be more work. Miss Kay agreed to see how this would progress and eventually the directors agreed that Miss Kay could check the wage books of the girls at the end of the year to see if the tailoresses had benefitted from this new system.[20] Once appointed as Organiser for the tailoresses the Council asked her to become a member and sit on their organising committee which was an important source of support for her with the two Organising Secretaries who agreed to support her with the work

17

OUTSIDE VIEW OF TAILORING FACTORY.

Broughton Tailoring Factory.

THIS department was established seven years ago, in 1892, and certainly up to the present has entirely justified the purpose for which it was started. As with other C.W.S. productive departments it has grown very rapidly, and already has had to be moved several times in order to obtain the requisite accommodation. The present factory at Broughton was opened in June, 1897. To anticipate further progress, the new factory was built for 800 employés, and already, within two years, there are nearly 500 people in regular employment. It is specially adapted to suit all the requirements of the tailoring trade, well-built, well-lighted, airy, and commodious. It has three floors and a basement. The top floor is used as a machine-room for coats, and in the winter season is given over entirely to the making of overcoats, of every style and weight—from the light covert coat to the heavy tweed ulster. The second floor is also used as a machine-room for vests, trousers, and knickers. At the end of each room there is a large number of finishers, seated on each side of two long benches, who are busily engaged button-holing, sewing on buttons, tacking, felling lin and innumerable other little jobs which are as important to the worth of the article and comfort of the wearer as the cutting or machi or even the pressing. There are nearly 200 w and girls on each of these floors. Our illustr is of the coat machine-room. On the first flo find the offices, the stockrooms, the cutting-r and the tailors' workshop. The long cutting-r with its numerous cutting-tables and its two knives, gives a very favourable impression c capacity of the establishment. There are als other cutting-rooms in the bays. In the base are the two large gas engines, the mechanics' the kitchen, and the two dining-rooms—one fo men and one for the women—and also some stockrooms.

We could not fail to observe that the cla girls employed is superior to those we see co away from some of the clothing factories he Manchester. We have not far to search reason for this. Doing a superior class of the management are able to pay a better wage thus they have the opportunity to select a sup class of workpeople, thus ensuring first-class

BROWNFIELDS POTTERY GUILD.—Agents, C.W.S.

CWS Broughton factory. Image courtesy of the Co-operative archive at the CWS and in contacting workers about the effect of the new system.

The work of organising tailoresses was often difficult. In the ASTT journal Mr. Alf H. Casbon, Secretary of the Bury Branch, reported that they had invited one of the organising secretaries of the MSWTUC, Mrs. Dickenson, to support them in recruiting tailoresses in local shops. She had then spoken at a meeting but only eight women attended. After the meeting Mr. Casbon followed up contacts but the women did not respond. He recognised the importance of recruiting the women into the trade but castigated the male tailors for not encouraging their daughters or sisters to join.

With regard to the organising of women, this is a little history. I wish we could report as favourably as upon the men's organisation. The commencement dates from last autumn and the coming down of Mrs. Dickenson from Manchester, visiting the shops, and finally addressing a meeting in the Textile Hall, at which seven or eights tailoresses attended. Then I invited them to attend a meeting at my house, sent postcards, circularised and stopped them in the street and gave a general invitation but am sorry to say that not one came.

This somewhat dampened our ardour, but still we have been pegging away ever since Christmas, and apparently the net result of all this is – one of our members started paying for his sister, with the hope that if we could only get to start it would an inducement for others to join, which leaves us in a very similar position to my friend Mr.Lynch of Dunbarton.

We shall not have to give up with this little reverse or want of success, but go in again, for it is my firm conviction – and of many others with me – and has been for years, that they will have to be organised. They are in trade, and all they earn is got in the trade, and as trade unionists it would be somewhat illogical to attempt to oust them. But perhaps the actual result must not be counted by the number of members obtained, or the want of them.

There is a great deal of educational work to be done, and this is a very slow process, as they will find out who engage it; a great deal of opposition to breakdown and prejudice to overcome and from quarters least expected. Our own members are very tardy, in compelling their daughters to join, and by so doing are offering a very effective opposition.

Trade unionists with daughters, and even unionist secretaries, when waited up to use their influence, reply "If they like to join I will offer no opposition, but they can please themselves.. Forgetting at the same time, that even threepence per week is a consideration to a young girl, after she has handed her wages over to her parents, and gets sixpence or a shilling back for pocket money; also that any benefits derived – out of work, sick pay and increased wages – will accrue to them, and that if sickness comes they have to keep them, and nothing at all coming in. This may seem more verbiage, but it will perhaps put anyone who is about to undertake this part of trade unionism up to a stripe or two. They will find it a labour of love, and right as them to be instant in season or out.[21]

In her interview in the ASTT journal Miss Kay also explained how difficult it was to organise the women:

A combination of causes operate against us. First, the trade is somewhat complicated in its working. For instance, it has a slack and a busy period. It is never a constant, steady employment. In the busy times the girls won't join us, and in the slack times they very often cannot, on account of their meagre earnings, which won't allow of deductions of union subscriptions. Then, again, dismissal is often the penalty a girl has to pay who joins us. Mrs. Dickenson, I believe, gave you an idea of how we go to work. We visit the girls at their workshops during the dinner-hour, and also arrange for public meetings to be held in the evenings.[22]

In work the women worked long hours which contravened the limited labour laws that existed:
In many workshops the hours are shockingly long, though the legal hours are from 8-30a.m. to 6p.m., with an hour for dinner. But the law is often set at naught. I have heard of girls working till 2,3, and even until 6 o'clock in the morning during the busy season. Others again start at 6 o'clock instead of 8-30; and the girls are given to understand that if the inspector should inquire they must declare they started at the later hour.[23]

Tailoresses who worked from home were even more exploited:
They have to find their own machine, cotton, and light. And although some of the work is done in fairly decent neighbourhoods, the majority of the home-workers are in the poorer districts.

Besides finding their own machines and cotton, these women have to fetch the material from the workshop, and also to carry back the finished article; nothing is given for this. But the system of buying the cotton is not confined to the out-workers; employees inside some of the workshops have to pay as much as 3d. a reel for their thread. They are bound, too, to purchase from their employer, although they could obtain the same quality and quantity of cotton outside for 2d. per reel. That is really wrong, although by compelling the employees to sign a paper respecting fines, etc, when they commence working for him, the employer places himself out of the reach of the law.[24]

Miss Kay had worked in different parts of the tailoring industry in Manchester; from the large and generally respected CWS to private firms and workshops. One aspect she does comment on is the difference between Jewish and Christian tailors. This is without clarifying her own ethnicity.

"The Jews," she observed, "often work on quite a different system to the Christian tailors. It is difficult to explain to an outsider, but their trade is a medium between the wholesale and the private trade system. They are often engaged on day work; and employers often make this system a means of getting labour cheap: as he will run, say, one-and-half-days' work into one day.

Generally speaking, Jews work at cheaper rates and longer hours than Christians. Many of them jump into the trade with scarcely any training. In the wholesale trade their is no real system of apprenticeship; and I know of Russian Jews, who have been blacksmiths in their native land, on arriving in England have become tailors. That is why their labour is so much cheaper than Christian tailors."[25]

Miss Kay's organising work was paying off but in April 1902 it was reported at a Council meeting that:
... the Tailoresses were steadily increasing their membership but unfortunately the Amalgamated Society of Tailors had decided to discontinue the organising work, & suggested that Miss Kay should go back to tailoring now that the trades was busy. The Council expressed its regret & instructed Mrs. Dickenson to see Mr. Flynn (ASTT) about the matter.[26]

A compromise was agreed and the following month the minutes recorded:
The matter was discussed by the Council and it was decided that in view of the good work done by Miss Kay for the Society an effort should be made to retain her services for at least another year. It was arranged that the Secretaries should find out if it was possible to come to an agreement with the Amalgamated Society of Tailors & Tailoresses by which this society should guarantee £26 towards Miss Kay's salary. If the agreement could be satisfactorily arranged it was decided to start a separate fund to raise the rest of the money. That no time might be lost, the Secretaries were empowered to close with the Tailors' Society subject to the approval of Miss Bulley and to ask Miss Kay to resume the organising work at once. It was considered impossible to ask her to leave her present work, unless a year's salary £52 was guaranteed. It was thought that this fund might be raised by private contributions and grants from Women's Trade Unions."

Miss Kay thus continued her work recruiting and organising members and taking up the cases of exploited tailoresses. In the ASTT Journal dated 15th August 1902 it was recorded that there were now 99 members of the Manchester Tailoresses branch.

In December 1902 Miss Kay reported to the Council that they had had "a very successful meeting at Shamrock Hall. There were over 100 present. The meeting was mainly of a social character, but speeches were made and many of those present promised to join after Christmas."[28]

Miss Kay was also involved with the attempts by the MSWTUC to get a representative on Manchester City Council's Education Committee which had replaced the School Board.

...Mrs. Dickenson reported that she and Miss Kay had again interviewed Sir James Hay and Mr. Reynolds, with very satisfactory results. The matter was discussed, and Miss Rowlette moved "that the Council formally endorse the nomination of the candidate of the Combined Committee of the Women's Unions (Miss Gore-Booth) for the Education Committee of the Manchester Town Council."[29]

Miss Kay's job as organiser for the Tailoresses came to an end in May 1903 when the Minutes reported that "that the 12 months was over for which the Tailoresses Special Organiser was employed. The question of renewal was discussed. The Committee expressed their appreciation of Miss Kay's hard work & enthusiasm, but at the same time decided that for financial reasons it was impossible to renew the appointment for the present."[30]

JOURNAL

OF THE AMALGAMATED SOCIETY OF Tailors & Tailoresses.

THE OFFICIAL ORGAN OF THE SOCIETY.

Published by the Secretary, to whom all communications should be addressed, at the Offices of the Society, 415, Oxford Street, Manchester.

Masthead of the Journal of the Amalgamated Society of Tailors & Tailoresses

The Annual Report for 1903 recorded: "It is not too much to say that during the time of her employment she canvassed every shop of any importance in the district.[31]

After this she slips out of sight until the autumn of 1904 when there was a split in the Council. Eva Gore Booth and Sarah Dickenson resigned from the MSWTUC in protest because the Council Committee refused to add women's suffrage to their aims. They then set up another organisation: the Manchester and Salford Women's Trades and Labour Council. A bitter row then broke out over the nomination to the Manchester Education Committee which exposed the divide between the two organisations.

Miss Kay and the Tailoresses had taken the side of the suffragists and joined the new Council, publicly announcing this as a signatory to a letter to the *Manchester Guardian* on 11th November 1904. Alongside other trade union women - including Nellie Keenan, Sarah Dickenson, Evelyn Tonkin, Isabel Forsyth and Violet Whalley- Miss Kay stated that as a result of a radical difference of opinion between the Trades Council and the trade unions, they had decided to withdraw:

They were convinced that the time had come when it was essential for the unions' progress and future development that they should stand on an independent and self-reliant basis and formulate their own policy. A representative Women's Trades and Labour Council was therefore constituted. It will be seen that this Council is not in the real sense a new and untried body, as it is formed from the representative sof the most important and long-established unions. The Women's Trades and Labour Council wish to protest most strongly against the nomination of a working women's represenative by the Manchester and Salford and District Women's Trades Council.

Miss Gore-Booth was chosen by the women trade-unionists to be their representative, and they are quite satisfied with her, and do not want wish for a change. Miss Emily Cox, who is now supposed to represent them, was nominated without any woman trade-unionist in the city being consulted. With all due respect to Miss Emily Cox, who, we have no doubt, is a most worthy lady, she has no claim whatever to represent the women's trade unions of this district.

The Manchester and Salford Women Trades and Labour Council strongly deprecates that this nomination should be in the hands of any philanthropic body, no matter how well intentioned.[32]

Unfortunately there are no surviving Minute Books of the MSWTLC so we do not know for how long Miss Kay carried on as Secretary of the Tailoresses' Society. We do know that by 1907 the Secretary is a Miss Preston. Perhaps Miss Kay got married or even emigrated for a better life.

The story of Miss Kay reflects the lives of many women – in the past and today – who refuse to accept being treated as a second class worker and seize the opportunity to join with other women and men to improve her conditions at work through joining a trade union and becoming an activist.

I think she was fortunate that the MSWTUC existed to support and encourage her and to provide a women's only space where she could get support. I was lucky to track down an interview with her in the ASTT Journal and through her words (although edited) see a determined woman and strong trade unionist.

In the early 1900s women like Miss Kay were not just fighting for their rights at work but were facing sexism in their trade unions, and discrimination in the workplace. But they were living at an exciting time for women due to the actions of women workers such as the Matchwomen and the constant struggle going on for the vote for women.

Like many other women of this era Miss Kay saw that it was not enough to take on employers but that the struggle must include the issue of the vote if working class women were to gain equality in society.

Her name does not appear in any of the histories of the suffragist and suffragette movement. It is time that this changed.

"Fabric of Our Lives". Chicago Women's Labor mosaic by Miriam Socoloff and Cynthia Weiss, 1980

References

1   MSWTUC 1902 Annual Report. They raised £4. 2s from supporters to spend on tea. "Mrs. Hobhouse and Mrs. Spence Weiss kindly sent cake, and Mrs. Flynn a parcel of tea."

2   MSWTUC, 1903 Annual Report.

3   W. Elkin, "Manchester" in Married Women's Work, edited by Clementina Black (1913).

4   MSWTUC minutes, 7th December 1897.

5   Rosalyn D Livshin, Non-Conformity in the Jewish community: the case of Political Radicalism, 1889-1939, PhD, University of Manchester, 2015, p. 26.

6   MSWTUC minutes, 29th March 1898.

7   MSWTUC minutes, 28Th October 1898.

8   Tailor and Cutter, 8th July 1899.

9   Manchester Evening News, 10th July 1899, p.3.

10   MSWTUC Annual Report 1900.

11   MSWTUC Annual Report 1900.

12   Interview with Miss Kay, Journal of the Amalgamated Society of Tailors and Tailoresses Vol.1, No. 8. January 1902

13   Interview with Miss Kay, Journal of the Amalgamated Society of Tailors and Tailoresses Vol.1, No. 8. January 1902

14   Interview with Miss Kay, Journal of the Amalgamated Society of Tailors and Tailoresses Vol.1, No. 8. January 1902

15   Oldham Wheatsheaf, July 1899.

16   Oldham Industries Co-operative Society Record, June 1899.

17   Amalgamated Society of Tailors' Journal, October 1899.

18   MSWTUC minutes, 6th November 1900.

19   MSWTUC minutes, 3rd December 1901.

20   MSWTUC minutes, 10th September 1901, 5th November 1901.

21   Journal of the Amalgamated Society of Tailors and Tailoresses Vol.1, 4th September 1901.

22   Interview with Miss Kay, Journal of the Amalgamated Society of Tailors and Tailoresses Vol.1, No. 8. January 1902.

23   Interview with Miss Kay, Journal of the Amalgamated Society of Tailors and Tailoresses Vol.1, No. 8. January 1902.

24   Interview with Miss Kay, Journal of the Amalgamated Society of Tailors

and Tailoresses Vol.1, No. 8. January 1902.

25   Interview with Miss Kay, Journal of the Amalgamated Society of Tailors and Tailoresses Vol.1, No. 8. January 1902

26   MSWTUC minutes, 8th April 1902.

27   MSWTUC minutes, 6th May 1902.

28   MSWTUC minutes, 2nd December 1902.

29   MSWTUC minutes, 3rd February 1903.

30   MSWTUC minutes, 26th May 1903.

31   MSWTUC, 1903 Annual report.

32   Manchester Guardian, 11th November 1904

Interview with Miss Kay, of the A.S.T.

SOME weeks ago I promised our readers to try to secure an interview with Miss Nellie Kay, organising secretary of the tailoresses' branch of the Amalgamated Society of Tailors and Tailoresses in Manchester, with the object of learning something of the working lives of the large number of women and girls engaged in the tailoring trade. I have been successful ; for in reply to my request Miss Kay readily agreed to meet me and give me all the information she could respecting the society which she represents and the work which she is engaged in.

I went to Manchester and spent an hour with Miss Kay ; and came away after our interview filled with indignation ; my feelings of anger roused by the recital of the sufferings, the wrongs and the general unhappy conditions under which thousands of women and girls in Manchester toil.

It is nearly sixty years since the poet, Thomas Hood, wrote his famous " Song of the Shirt " ; a poem drawing attention to the hard, bitter lives of the sempstresses in London ; a poem, too, of which it was said that it had done more towards bringing about an improvement in the lot of the London sweated shirtmakers than any agitation. I would that a song of the tailoress-made coat could be written which would have a similar effect to T m Hood's poem ; only that Manchester as well as London should be affected. There is need for inquiry into the conditions surrounding the lives of the tailoresses of our first Lancashire city.

Miss Kay is a Manchester woman, and since the age of sixteen has been engaged in the tailoring trade. " My family," she said, " have been tailors for generations, so I ought to know something about the trade."

" Now, Miss Kay," I said, " I would like to know, first of all, something about your society and its work."

" Well," she replied, " there is not a great deal to say about the Society ; that is, the women's branch. It is this branch which I represent, although we are amalgamated with the Tailors' Society. We only began about 2½ years ago, and we have about 100 members. In the city and district there are about 50 workshops—great and small—and we estimate the number of women and girl-workers in the tailoring trade between 4,000 and 5,000."

" Not a very large membership compared with the numbers employed," I observed.

" No," was Miss Kay's answer, " but it is very hard, uphill work trying to induce the girls to join."

" What are the main obstacles in your way ?" I asked.

" A combination of causes operate against us," she replied. First, the trade is somewhat complicated in its working. For instance, it has a slack and a busy period. It is never a constant, steady employment. In the busy time the girls won't join us, and in the slack time they very often cannot, on account of their meagre earnings, which won't allow of deductions for union subscriptions. Then, again, dismissal is often the penalty a girl has to pay who joins us. Mrs. Dickenson, I believe, gave you an idea of how we go to work. We visit the girls at their workshops during the dinner-hour, and also arrange for public meetings to be held in the evenings."

" Now, Miss Kay," I said, " I want you to tell me something regarding the lives of tailoresses — their working-lives, I mean. How are they treated in the matter of wages, hours, and their surroundings ?"

" In many workshops," she replied, " the hours are shockingly long, though the legal hours are from 8-30 a.m. to 6 p.m., with an hour for dinner. But the law is often set at naught. I have heard of girls working till 2, 3, and even until 6 o'clock in the morning during the busy season. Others again start at 6 o'clock instead of 8-30 ; and the girls are given to understand that if the inspector should inquire they must declare they started at the later hour."

" But do the girls give these false statements ?" I inquired.

" They do," replied Miss Kay. " It would mean loss of employment if they told the truth."

" What wages do they get for these hours ?" I then asked.

" In the busy season expert hands can earn 25s. per week," was Miss Kay's answer. " It very rarely happens that a tailoress gets more than that, while in the slack season a woman may receive 2s., and will have been every day to see if there was any work for her to do."

" How long does the busy season last ?" I queried.

"The greatest enemy to freedom is not the tyrant but the contented slave": When Kitty met David...

by Georgina Gittins

This article is the result of my research into Kitty Marion, one of three suffragettes seriously assaulted by the crowd after heckling Lloyd George at the National Eisteddfod of Wales, 1912, which was held in Wrexham, my home town. I was shocked at the scale of the assault and wondered why I had never heard about it?

In Wrexham, public meetings addressed by national and local politicians were regularly held and well attended; the public seemed to like to hear policy "from the horse's mouth," and heckling was commonplace, by men *and* women. Using Kitty as a representative of the wider suffragette movement, I wanted to discover why the suffragettes provoked such a violent response, and learn how they maintained their mental health in the face of such hostility.

Childhood
Kitty was born Katherine Maria Shäfer, in Dortmund, Germany in 1871. When she was two years old her mother and baby brother died from tuberculosis. Her father and stepmother subjected Kitty to an abusive childhood, from calling her red hair ugly to breaking her nose. She was never trusted, always punished; never heard, always silenced. Kitty had to conform to her father's rules, curtailing all freedoms; as a result, she experienced periods of feeling an

"unfathomable sense of depression" as well as a child's "high spirited happiness." Her dreams of serving as a soldier or an engineer were out of the question to women, while her ambition to sing on the stage was ridiculed: she should not draw attention to herself.

Kitty decided not to marry as she never wanted to be told she was 'a burden' again, and, although she loved the company of children, she did not want to bring any into such an unjust world.

In 1886, following an invitation from her aunt, Kitty sailed to England without telling her father. She was 15, and spoke no English. She took dancing lessons - "imperfect speech would not handicap dancing" – and found work and lodgings.

Independence
Kitty's bold move allowed her to emerge from her crushing childhood into an independent young woman; her only wish was to support herself as a singer and dancer in music halls, pantomimes, and shows while learning English.

The next pivotal event of her life took place in the office of a junior partner she nicknamed Mr 'Dreck,' the German word for 'filth' or 'smut.' Kitty resisted his sexual assault, during which time she hit her head on a table and lost consciousness. She told no-one about the incident until she wrote about it in her autobiography during the 1930s; instead Kitty hit the depths of despair and considered drowning herself before her desire to avenge the insult recovered her determination.[1]

Sex governed work; refusal of sex to men resulted in Kitty being told that her work was "not satisfactory" and her contract terminated. Promotion to leading roles was not on merit, but dependent on being 'kept' by a wealthy, important man. I wonder how Kitty would react to being told that it would take until 2016 for these issues to be taken seriously via the "Me Too" movement.

"I wondered sometimes why life was made so difficult for women; what was the use of struggling on when the odds were all against one, why not end it all with one plunge?" But her mood improved when she thought of all her friends, fighting the same battles; she determined that "somehow, I would fight this vile, economic and sex domination over women which has no right to be, and which no man or woman worthy of the term should tolerate." Her friends would prove to be very important at such times of stress.

Kitty neatly summarised how layers of unfairness in society are perpetuated when she complained to a landlady about bedbugs; the landlady told her that "she must have brought them with her." Kitty showed her the bugs behind the wallpaper, at which the landlady apologised explaining that "no one had ever complained before." These six words underpinned the "accumulation of wrongs humanity is suffering from," wrote Kitty.

Becoming a campaigner

Kitty's first fight back, in 1906 was to join a union; the Variety Artists Federation (VAF), which fought for better conditions for music hall workers. It was later incorporated into the actor's union, Equity. She lost more contracts when organisers refused to recruit VAF members. During the six-week Great Music Hall Strike of 1907 Kitty paid into strike funds, wrote to newspapers and was stirred by joining picket lines and listening to speakers. Many friends refused to join her, telling her she should be satisfied with whatever she had, and could only blame herself for losing work.

In June 1908 she joined the Actor's Association contingent of a rally organised by the Women's Social and Political Union (WSPU). Listening to rally speakers was another pivotal moment for Kitty. More layers of injustice to women were laid bare. "Being deprived of a voice in the government to which they were subservient; of having to pay taxes in the expenditure of which they had no voice, the inequality between the sexes before the law regarding divorce, the ownership of legitimate and so-called illegitimate children, the difference between the sexes regarding conditions and payment in the labour market, the difference in punishment for similar crimes committed, and so forth." She felt as if the scales were falling from her eyes: "Well, now I was awake. I was one of them and would do all I could to help and make our dream of a better world come true."

As a single woman earning her own living without the influence or protection of a man, Kitty experienced the full force of entrenched sexual discrimination against women. She was economically abused in the workplace thanks to separate pay and conditions for men and women; sexually abused in the workplace where it was condoned by society; and, underpinning everything, politically abused by a society which made it impossible for her to change the laws perpetuating her position as she could not vote. She recognised "the contented slave" motto from the front page of *The Performer*, the VFA newspaper: "The greatest enemy to freedom is not the tyrant but the contented slave"[2]

Only a women's union would be able to take on such huge issues; thus Kitty joined the WSPU.

The words of David Lloyd George, the first Welsh cabinet minister resonated for her:
"There comes a time in the life of a people suffering from an intolerable injustice when the only way to maintain one's self-respect is to revolt against that injustice."[3]

Her double life began – campaigning for the WSPU and the VAF, and working in theatres.

Double life

Kitty began by selling Votes for Women in Piccadilly Circus, feeling as if "every eye that looked at me was a dagger piercing me through and [wishing] the ground would open and swallow me. However, that feeling wore off and I developed into quite a champion paper-seller."

In September 1909, Kitty was "incited to violence" after Mary Leigh was force-fed in Winson Green Goal, Birmingham. Mary's hunger strike was in protest at the government's refusal to recognise suffragettes as political prisoners; the government's escalation of the issue resonated with Kitty as being "symbolic of beating a woman into submission" –

Double life[4]

which is what Kitty's father had done to her.[5]

Her activism began in Newcastle, where Lloyd George, the Chancellor of the Exchequer, addressed male-only taxpayers about the Budget. She agreed to throw a stone through the window of a post office at 7pm to coincide with his talk. Feeling "deadly sick and nervous," and having thoroughly searched the building to ensure no-one would be injured by falling glass, she found herself "waiting for the stroke of the clock, which seemed as if it would never strike again." The clock did strike; the window was smashed, and a nearby crowd cheered and shouted, "Votes for Women!" Kitty was arrested, pleaded guilty, and was sentenced to one month's hard labour, telling the court that she was only practising what Lloyd George had preached.[6]

She refused food in accordance with WSPU policy of seeking political recognition for prisoners. She gave a graphic account of being restrained and force-fed in prison in a room with three doctors and wardresses:

I refused and was seized and overpowered by several wardresses, forced into an armchair, covered by a sheet, each arm held to the arm of the chair by a wardress, two others holding my shoulders back, two more holding my knees down, a doctor holding my head back.

I struggled and screamed all the time. Not knowing the procedure of forcible feeding and thinking it was done through the mouth, I clenched my teeth when they had me in position and helpless, when suddenly I felt something penetrate my right nostril which seemed to cause my head to burst and eyes to bulge.

Choking and retching as the tube was forced down to the stomach and the liquid food poured in, most of which was vomited back especially when the tube was withdrawn. There are no words to describe the horrible revolting sensations. I must have lost consciousness for I found myself flat on the floor, not knowing how I got there. When wardresses were picking me up to carry me back to my cell, I heard one say, "Eh but she's heavy!" I said, "Of course, I am. Put me down, I'll walk back, they would leave work like this for you women to do.

I called the doctors a lot of dirty, cringing doormats to the government to lend themselves to such outrageous treatment of women." [7]

As I write this, in January 2022, most people will know the discomfort of putting a covid swab up into their nostril; scale up the discomfort by imagining inserting a rubber tube instead.

Kitty protested at her treatment by setting fire to her cell.

For the next two years, Kitty took part in WSPU militant campaigns resulting from the failure of two Bills to pass through Parliament which would have enfranchised women. She was one of 119 women arrested at "Black Friday," a peaceful deputation to Downing Street following the failure of the Conciliation Bill in 1910 at which women were subjected to brutality and sexual abuse meted out by plain-clothed and uniformed police as described by Mrs Georgiana Solomon in her letter of complaint to her MP, Herbert Gladstone.

A number of the police pushed me, and literally threw me, from one batch of them to another, in the Parliament Square.

At last, in a still more powerful rush of the police, one of them flung me ruthlessly backwards prone on the ground. Then the group of them looked a little bit frightened. Some ladies came to minister to me, and raised my head. I had a kind message afterwards through Lady Balfour from her sister Lady Constance Lytton (herself sadly hurt and fainting. I felt so sorry to see her plight!) who said she had witnessed with great regret the way in which I was treated. Others also saw it.

I had been begging and praying for a few moments respite just to get my breath, but all in vain.

As I lay on the ground, and after I arose, I asked again and again by whose commands women were treated thus in a free country like our England? And why they were so cruel and merciless to an old lady like myself? - being now over sixty-four. But no answer was given.

As soon as I had staggered to my feet, it was only to be driven before many policemen, dragged by the arms, and shunted in every direction, my dress being torn by them, and every part of my being vibrating from the effects of shock and painful usage. No quarter was granted. But, all the time, as many of the populace as could get at all were joined in my request in a Three Cheers for "Votes for Women!" I did not forget our cause.[8]

Two window-smashing demonstrations then followed in protest at the failure of the second Bill. In November 1911, 223 women were arrested for breaking windows in The Strand and government buildings in Whitehall; Kitty broke a window in the Home Office and received a short sentence.

The second window-smashing demonstration was on an unprecedented scale, taking place on St David's Day 1912, another attempt to influence Lloyd George. That evening, 150 windows in the main shopping streets of London were smashed at the same time in a highly co-ordinated campaign. Kitty explained the operation: "Each, separately, in a private room, was given a hammer and told which windows to break at 5:45 P.M. in the twilight and lighting-up time when people had finished shopping and were peacefully wending their way home." Kitty's targets were the windows of the Silversmiths' Association and Sainsbury's; she was one of 126 women arrested.

Photograph of tube used for orally force-feeding prisoners in Walton Gaol. Photograph: Georgina Gittins, Taking Liberties display, Museum of Liverpool.

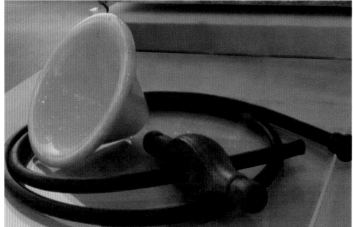

Kitty was sentenced to six months hard labour and taken to Winson Green Gaol where she was force-fed then released after 10 days.[9]

Two sisters from Lancashire, Margaret E and Mary D Thompson, also convicted of taking part in the campaign, wrote in their account of their treatment *They Couldn't Stop Us* that they appreciated hearing Kitty singing to everyone to keep up their morale: "At one time Kitty Marion began to sing. This was pleasing, but she was not allowed to go on for long."[10]

Her ticket for the Eisteddford from her scrapbook

The National Eisteddfod of Wales, 1912

Kitty's next protest would take her to Wrexham, where she was to heckle Lloyd George at the National Eisteddfod of Wales. She explained why. "Since Cabinet Ministers guarded themselves at their own meeting against being questioned by women, by keeping the latter out, they went to wherever else a Minister appeared, to heckle him with pertinent questions on women's suffrage." Her ticket is shown here from her scrapbook; she sat near to the stage, where she and Lloyd George would have had good views of each other.[11]

Eisteddfod are festivals of literary and musical competitions, and of great importance to Welsh culture and so Wrexham Council had worked hard to prepare Bellevue Park to host the Eisteddfod. Since it hardly features in history books, I'd like to describe the event from all standpoints, and then its fallout.

Lloyd George addressed its culminating event, the Chairing of the Bard ceremony. It was the busiest day, with press reports estimating around 13,000 people present, with many others unable to gain entrance. Lloyd George was adored in Wrexham and this was by no means his first visit; many had come to hear Wales' first Cabinet Minister speak. When news of his arrival travelled through the crowd the performers on stage were drowned by jubilant cheers, and when he arrived on the stage the crowd gave him an ovation lasting for several minutes, throwing their handkerchiefs into the air and waving frantically, before resuming their seats to listen to his address. But to their anger, he was interrupted by a woman shouting, "Why don't you give women their rights?" The *Wrexham Advertiser* vividly described the scene.

For a moment the situation looked ugly, the crowd swayed, but the barriers were too strong. The interrupter was very quickly ejected and there was great commotion. Before the Chancellor could proceed a man was foolish enough to express himself in sympathy with the women's cause, and he was forcibly ejected and left to the tender mercies of the crowd outside. It was some time before the crowd could be got under control again.

The band struck up a Welsh air and order eventually resumed. But now it was Kitty's turn.

The Chancellor proceeded, but had not spoken half a dozen sentences when a woman with auburn hair jumped up and asked, "How dare you force feed women." Again, there was an ugly rush in her direction, but the woman was fortunately surrounded by stewards and police and rushed out of the building. She lost "a quantity of her hair" from the "angry" audience and another man "with an imperial beard" asked why women should not have the vote – he was attacked, and the barriers could be heard breaking above the noise of the crowd.

The Chancellor looked on but did not look the least perturbed, and presently he again essayed to continue his speech."

But Lloyd George was interrupted one final time by a woman asking him to "do your duty to Englishwomen.":

The crowd dealt with her "less kindly" than they had the others, while outside, the large crowd was waiting to pounce on each suffragette as she was ejected, and the stewards acted very wisely in detaining them in a room at the rear of the platform.

The band played the Welsh National Anthem after each interruption in an attempt to calm the "violent hands" of the crowd, but the scene outside of the Pavilion was actually more dangerous.

The hundreds of people unable to gain admission were waiting round the doors, and as the suffragettes were ejected, they were immediately surrounded by the crowd. Their hats were torn off, blouses and clothing torn, and, to say the least, they were very roughly handled. The police did all in their power, but they were helpless against such odds. The male sympathiser was struck about the face and body and also kicked. The struggling man received a nasty smack in the eye which immediately closed up and became very discoloured. The suffragettes were buffeted all about the place. Eventually the police succeeded in getting four of them into a room at the rear of the platform. For a considerable time, a large crowd waited outside for the Suffragettes to come out, and the latter would undoubtedly have received brutal treatment if they had not received this protection. Clothing and hats had to be provided before the women could leave the room.[12]

Victim's experiences

Kitty devoted pages 4 – 8 of her scrapbook to press reports on the Eisteddford. Her own testimony echoes the descriptions in the local and national press.

Within ten minutes I experienced all the concentrated essence of coarse brutalities and indecencies of several hours' battle in Westminster.

Thirty minutes of Wrexham's fury[13]

I jumped up and shouted, "How dare you have political prisoners fed by force!" Pandemonium reigned once more. I was seized by a steward and policeman who hurried me to an exit while I received blows and abuse from every side, my hat being torn off and hair pulled down. Outside a dense, howling mob almost tore me to pieces. My hair was grabbed and pulled out by the roots. Quoting myself from "Votes for Women," September 13th 1912: "My clothes were ripped back and front, my very undergarments torn to shreds. Being thrown to wild beasts is nothing to being thrown to an infuriated human mob. The former might tear you to pieces but draw the line at indecent assaults, and so do I. I don't mind the cuffs, kicks, blows, aches and pains a man might get in such a struggle.

The police somehow forced a passage from the side of the building to the stage entrance and safety at the back. It was a ghastly, vile experience which each one of us went through. All

the veneer of man's vaunted civilization vanished at woman's demand for justice and fair play.

Amongst the hecklers was a man, "a Colonial", on a visit to his Mother country after twenty years absence, who protested against the brutal treatment of the women. For his chivalry, he was thrown out, badly beaten and his eyes blackened. He told the Press, "I have fought for my country but never with such savages as I encountered today." [14]

I can only find one comment about how Kitty was affected by the brutality. Eighteen months after the Eisteddfod, she wrote to suffragette friend Rachel Peace on a piece of prison toilet paper, enclosing a lock of her hair:

'The Lock.' I used to have great quantities of it, but crimping irons, (illegible), and the 'Wrexham Eisteddfod' 18 months ago have played havoc with it. It is falling out dreadfully here. It used to be like a thick cloak round me and I could sit on it, but now there seems to be little but the 'fast' die (sic) left. Sic transit Gloria Mundi."[15]

An outraged article in *Votes for Women* carried Kitty's account, testimony from witnesses, including locals, and from the "Colonial," who expressed his disillusionment with Britain compared to the colony he had returned from where women had the vote and were treated with courtesy. He felt "shock and horror" at how they were treated in their campaign for citizenship and "in the sweating dens of all her great cities," which compelled him to stand up and shout, "Why do you refuse to give women the vote? You daren't because you'll lose a fund of sweated labour, on which you must draw to make your sweated products."[16]

Kitty wrote that the Pethick-Lawrences resigned from WSPU in September 1912 over the level of danger women in the campaign were exposed to.[17]

Non-Suffragette Responses
Their target, Lloyd George, had it within his power to call the crowd to desist. The caption above his photograph in her scrapbook reflected his statement to the crowd: "They were insulting a whole nation." He reminisced about past Eisteddfod competitions "for a wooden spoon, and for the best ash walking stick. They could do that afternoon with one of those walking sticks or with the wooden spoon."

"Mr. Lloyd George Incites to Violence" was the bold headline of an article in *Votes for Women* giving eye-witness accounts of the outcome of his response to the suffragette protests.

Here was a festival of music and poetry, and here came the cabinet minister who owes an explanation to the women of the country. Their frank questions were met by a most brutal treatment, which we know would never have been meted out had not a remark in the course of his interrupted speech been taken as a direct incitement to violence.[18]

The Denbighshire Constabulary must be recognised for their efforts to rescue protestors, in stark contrast to that of the Metropolitan Police, who received their instructions from the government. Wrexham's Mayor, Councillor W J Williams stated that "there might have been loss of life had it not been for the police." Twenty Constables, a Sergeant and Inspector were on duty. [19]

Kitty explained that the suffragettes were escorted to the station by "sympathetic detectives" at dusk. On her return to London, friends already knew what had happened:

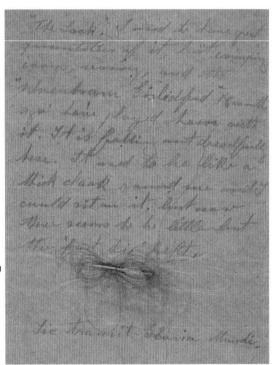

Remembering Wrexham

**"Oh, Aunt Kate, you're all over the town, looking awful!" And there they were outside of all the news dealers, large posters of me between two policemen, laughing at a "lady" who was yelling at me that I was "a disgrace to your sex," and looking cheerfully towards the safe heaven of the stage door we were approaching.
"Undaunted by the jeers of the onlookers" was the graceful caption the "Daily Sketch" gave it.**[20]

National response
Wrexham was certainly in the spotlight. The Eisteddfod was an important event; the National Press were there and published horrified accounts accompanied by photographs. Letters to the Editor of the *Daily Herald,* for instance, were amongst those who expressed shock at the way 'gallant little Wales' treated women and the way Lloyd George in Parliament had dismissed the press reports as "unutterable falsehood," (what we would call "fake news" to-day).[21]

The response from the National League for Opposing Women's Suffrage echoed that of "Mr Dreck" i.e., you will only face attack if you resist so it's your own fault! Capitalising on the Eisteddfod attacks, but avoiding Wrexham, they led a Holiday Campaign through North and West Wales during the summer of 1912 where membership blossomed from four North Wales branches to thirteen by December.[22]

Undaunted by the jeers of onlookers

The *Western Mail* echoed that responsibility for the attacks lay with the suffragettes: "though one readily confesses that the punishment was hopelessly out of proportion on this particular occasion."[23]

Wrexham and 'the woman issue.'
Public anger towards militancy already stifled the suffrage debate in Wrexham. This anger originated from 1909 when Mrs. Pankhurst and a group of suffragettes heckled Lloyd George at that year's National Eisteddfod of Wales held at the Albert Hall, London.

Most Wrexham people didn't distinguish between militant and non-militant organisations. Consequently, when the non-militant National Union of Women's Suffrage Societies (NUWSS) toured North and Mid-Wales in summer 1909 their outdoor meetings were met by men with brickbats (pieces of brick from nearby brickworks) while indoor meetings were drowned by heckling. Women were constantly asked, "Why did you break up our Eisteddfod?"[24]

Non-militant voices were unheard until May 1911, when the newly-elected MP, Mr E T John invited members of the NUWSS Liverpool branch to hold a public meeting in Wrexham. Eleanor Rathbone and Maude Roydon came, inspiring the formation of a local Wrexham NUWSS branch.[25]

The branch keenly felt the effects of the 1912 Eisteddfod and the steady escalation of militancy thereafter. At their AGM in 1913 Mrs Agnes Aston stated "that if ever there was a time when they wanted all the encouragement and heartening they could get it was at present." They resolved "We must give no-one an excuse for thinking that women's suffrage is necessarily identified with violence." Each of their press releases carried the statements "law-abiding" and "non-militant" in an attempt to draw public attention away from militancy and towards the suffrage issue itself.[26]

Wales shows its teeth. (Cartoon from *Anti-Suffrage Review*)

SHOWING HIS TEETH.

Effects on the Eisteddfod of 1913

There were repercussions for the National Eisteddfod of Wales in 1913 when it was held in Abergavenny, Monmouthshire, making a loss of £500. Lloyd George was invited along with the minister responsible for the force-feeding policy – Home Secretary Mr Reginald McKenna – the MP for North Monmouthshire, so the insurance costs to protect the pavilion were greatly increased along with the cost of hiring 80 additional police. Costs were not recouped as visitor numbers were reduced; even the caterers failed to recoup their costs of staff hire and perishable food.[27]

In the event, Lloyd George failed to attend, sending a last-minute telegram while Mr McKenna and the Earl of Plymouth took each other's speaking slots to avoid disturbances.[28]

Militancy escalated in 1913. Kitty explained that instead of deliberately courting arrest to publicise the cause, "the edict now went forth to 'do all the damage possible without being caught.'"

Miss Annie Kenney told a WSPU meeting "that the burning down of a railway station only cost a half-crown train fare." She concluded: "Let us do as much damage as ever we can to rouse up public opinion." WSPU meetings were met by hostile crowds, and newspaper reports feel as if they were written with gritted teeth.[29]

Kitty stated, "After four successful fires and escapes, something went wrong with the fifth." Her scrapbook has cuttings of four unsolved arson attacks. Fire caused over £1,000 damage to Croxley Green railway station whilst it was closed to the public; next day, its stationmaster received a Suffragette newspaper in the post with the explanation, "Afraid copy left got burnt."[30]

A mansion in St Leonard's called 'Levetleigh' was gutted by fire, three women escaping in a car being the police suspects.[31]

"Papers dealing with Votes for Women outrages were also scattered about upon the rails" near burning carriages at Cricklewood.[32]

Coaches of an empty train standing in sidings between Teddington and Hampton Wick stations were "burning furiously" by the time the Fire Brigade arrived. They extinguished the flames in time to save "packages of literature dealing with the Woman Suffrage movement. Newspaper cuttings of recent suffragette outrages were also found scattered about the train."[33]

Her fifth arson attack was carried out with Betty Giveen, who had joined WSPU after Black Friday. Together, they burned down the Grand Stand at Hurst Park Racecourse after a suggestion that it "would make a most appropriate beacon" as a salute to the protest made by Emily Wilding Davison at the 1913 Epsom Derby. Emily was, at this time, unconscious in hospital. Emily and Kitty had first met in Newcastle. The night before the Derby, Emily gave Kitty "a tiny green chamois purse containing a sovereign for 'munitions I might need soon.'" This sovereign was used to pay for the materials which burned down Hurst Park.

Kitty appears to have carried out these 'deeds' from a sense of duty. "Though it had its humours, I hated the whole wretched business; we all did, and would much rather have had the vote than do this sort of thing to get it, but we did our 'duty' as we saw it, much like soldiers on the principle of, 'Theirs not to reason why.'"

Detectives found evidence linking Kitty and Betty to the Racecourse; they were both sentenced to three years in prison. She noted with satisfaction that "the re-building of the race stands communed immediately, employing 150 men, some of whom were heard to say 'God bless the Suffragettes!'"[34]

Kitty was released from Holloway under the "Cat and Mouse" Act after five days refusal to eat or drink, being allowed under the Act to spend five days recovering under licence before being returned to prison. She was cared for at a nursing home used by WSPU supporters which provided sisterhood - an important network of physical and psychological support, as well as a means of avoiding being returned to prison; Kitty swapped clothes with a friend of similar build and escaped to Surrey.

Her autobiography editors believe that she then hints at responsibility for more arson attacks including Seafield House and Sefton Park Palm House in Liverpool, the cactus house at Alexandra Park, Manchester and a smashed window at a reception given for Prime Minister Asquith.[35]

Her period of freedom ended when she was recognised and rearrested in January 1914. To improve the recognition of suspects, the Home Office commissioned and distributed covert photographs of imprisoned suffragettes. These were Britain's first ever covert surveillance photographs, and can be seen at the National Portrait Gallery. Number 13 is Kitty's professional studio portrait.[36]

First covert surveillance photographs in the UK

Kitty was returned to Holloway, where she refused food and drink; she was force-fed 232 times in six weeks, losing 36 pounds in weight before being released on licence for six days. She recuperated at "Piney's" nursing home (of Nurse Catherine Pine, in Notting Hill) where she enjoyed visits and letters from her network of suffragette friends. "The genial co-operation of members, supporters and friends of the militant movement in taking care of "Mice" all over the country was one of the social wonders of the period." Could 'mice' have recuperated without this sisterhood?

It was the late spring of 1914.[37]

Deportation to America

On 4th August 1914 Britain declared war on Germany. Kitty was torn "between natural love of the Fatherland, and love of the people among whom I had lived for 28 years." WSPU campaigning ceased and the Home Secretary, Reginald McKenna deported her to America. She arrived in New York on 6th November 1915.

Despite letters of introduction and contacts, she found it impossible to get work because "the American stage was more than over-crowded with artists who had flocked over from all European counties since the beginning of the war." Stressed, she frightened her landlady by 'disappearing' but she had actually found work in a boarding house, getting on well with her Belgian employers. Maybe the break from campaigning was therapeutic. It ended when Kitty read about the arrest of Margaret Sanger under Section 1142 of the Penal Code which made it illegal to explain or provide contraception; Sanger's campaign aimed to make contraception legally available via clinics.

Kitty booked a ticket to hear Sanger speak about her campaign. They recognised her name and must have thought she was the answer to their prayers; they needed street sellers. Kitty sold *Birth Control Review* (BCR) in many areas, but mainly on the corner of Macy's. She made herself a shoulder bag to hold copies of BCR, and enjoyed the support from "the clean, young mind of a group of little urchins who called out, "aw! lookit the statya of liberty!"[38]

BCR included articles written by Kitty about the people she encountered. Many were reticent to engage with her as the issue was regarded as 'smut' or shameful. Many feared, as they were told by Clergy, that they would "burn in hell" if they did not

"Aw, lookit the Statya of Liberty!"[39]

continue having more children, that God would provide, that contraception tampered with nature. Many were misinformed, believing that only abortion could limit family numbers. Others believed that contraception would encourage immorality in young women. For these people, Kitty was a target; she was physically and verbally attacked.

To other people, Kitty was a figurehead; whenever she was attacked, they supported her, making her feel "more than compensated by wonderful compliments on my courage and perseverance" and becoming her new network of "comrades" who helped her to cope. She earned their support because she listened; her responses were truthful, open, respectful. She dignified the debate, normalised it by dispelling doubts, challenging misconceptions and prejudiced remarks. A letter from a reader stated that, "The cheerful ladylike manner in which Miss Marion conducts herself, as she holds aloft her message to the world, adds dignity to the movement and in addition, provides the means to thousands of men and women to hear of your work."[40]

Kitty wished that legislators could hear the stories she'd heard in support of contraception. People wanted to limit their family size, particularly if they already had ten children, believing it was a personal not an ideological decision; some people wanted to protect the mother's health, particularly if she had already suffered complications, or was coping with a disability.

Kitty was arrested and charged with obstruction and selling obscene literature nine times, serving a thirty-day sentence in "The Tombs" (Manhattan Detention Centre). Just as in *Votes for Women*, BCR used her arrests to make enticing copy; sales increased.

"Wherever the news of Miss Marion's arrest and imprisonment has spread it has brought wider, deeper interest in the cause for which she is suffering." [41]

Eight court appearances were dismissed by magistrates who found that BCR was not 'obscene' and obstruction not proven. Ironically, this led to newsagents being allowed to sell BCR and, following Sanger's retirement, the new Birth Control Board ended 'degrading' street-sales in 1930 during the Great Depression when people probably needed her the most. The magazine folded three years later.[42]

The frequent arrests, court appearances and attacks from the public inevitably took their toll on her; she was also arrested as a "German spy," initiating years of investigation before she became a naturalised American citizen in 1922.

By June 1920 she expressed symptoms of mental distress manifesting themselves in her body, as they often do; "Arguments with police always caused me most excruciating pain, as if I had been physically thrashed, and my backbone crumbling." She felt "the injustice of it here so preyed on my mind that I felt death would be preferable and I went away, leaving a note for Mrs Kennedy which gave the idea that I had committed suicide."

Again, 'disappearing' strengthened her spirits. She found accommodation in Monticello and duly contacted friends, who told her of the police search and report in the New York Times. [43]

She visited London in 1925 then travelled for three months visiting old friends. She heard a debate in the House of Commons; "Looking down from the gallery on Lady Astor's hat, I felt a great thrill of pride to have been one of the women who had forced open the doors for her and others."

In her farewell article for BCR she wrote, "One of Macy's departmental heads told me the store felt it was losing an old friend." The Board gave her $500 and a farewell luncheon as a send-off before she sailed to England in March 1930 to attend the unveiling of the statue of Emmeline Pankhurst.

The unveiling is described by Kitty:
The Unveiling, how can I describe it? Meeting the "Girls of the old brigade!!!", the changed attitude in the police who were most deferential to the "women voters." Even the weather was in harmony with the occasion, sunny and warm just for the day. The ceremony of unveiling Mrs Pankhurst's Statue by Mr. Stanley Baldwin, who as Prime Minister had signed the Woman Suffrage Bill, was most impressive. Music was supplied by the Metropolitan Police Band, Dame Ethel Smyth, looking gorgeous and imposing in her Doctor of Music robes, conducting her own "March of the Women," raised her baton, saying, "Well, gentlemen, you have 'conducted' me a few times, now I am going to conduct you."

At night there was a dinner given in honour of Mrs E.K. Marshall through whose efforts and influence the Statue was made, and placed in the gardens near the House of Lords. When I arrived at the dinner, I was placed at the speakers' table at Mrs Marshall's right. I had not anticipated such honour and felt proud as a peacock with his tail spread.[44]

The Great Depression greeted her on her return. She found work with the Women's Peace Society, fighting the threats of war and fascism. Despite huge support, no money was forthcoming so it was disbanded in 1934.

And with this Kitty drew her autobiography to an end, reflecting on her "metamorphosis from a German militarist to an international pacifist." But her final comment expresses a dichotomy; she saw

her future "at times very uncomfortable, at other times 'ganz gemütliche' knees of the Gods." The German phrase refers to a state of cosiness or comfort similar to 'hygge,' reflecting a destiny in the hands of forces which could bring discomfort or contentment. Kitty failed to find a publisher for her autobiography.

Kitty's last ten years are known to us through two sources; correspondence with her support network - her suffragette and Birth Control friends, and an article in The New Yorker.

She found work with the Works Progress Administration (WPA) which was set up in 1935 to provide work during the Depression; she taught English to children of 'foreign' parents via the Speech Improvement Project. The New Yorker described how "she treats all her pupils as if they were future Presidents of the United States. When we asked her if that went for the little girls, too, Miss Marion was prompt in her reply. "Certainly," she said firmly. "There will be a woman President some day. I think it will be a good thing." She kept in touch with some of the children until her death in 1944.[45]

This work ended in 1936. Kitty joined The WPA Theatre Project, which ended in 1937 by which time letters suggest her mobility was deteriorating.

Kitty lived in the Margaret Sanger Nursing Home between 1938 and her death in 1944. She remained resilient, collecting newspaper cuttings for letters to her friends Edith How-Martyn and Alice Park, signing off on one occasion "with affectionate, suffragetty love."

Obituaries appeared in the *New York Herald* and *New York Times* and her death was acknowledged in the British press. Her wishes were for no funeral or flowers so her friends celebrated her life by displaying her mementos, reading from her 'diary,' and tributes, which were received from all over the world.[46]

References
[1] Gardner, V. and Atkinson, D. (eds), (2019) *Kitty Marion Actor and Activist,* Manchester University Press, (2019). p. 43. This book is the first publication of Kitty Marion's autobiography, which she completed in 1930. The Editors provide detailed annotations giving context and explanations to her text and use letters and newspaper reports to outline her final decade, which is not included in her autobiography. A description of her memorial celebration concludes the book.

Two Appendices include extracts from her Prison records and letters from Prison, and a third includes extracts from Home Office documents regarding her deportation to America. The bibliography fully explains all archival and published sources used. The book is edited by Viv Gardner, a performance historian and Diane Atkinson, a suffrage historian.

2 Motto on the front page of *The Performer*, the newspaper of The Variety Artistes Federation. It was also inscribed on the hammer Kitty used to smash a fire alarm in Covent Garden: *The Suffragette*, 27.12.1912 p 9, "False Fire Alarms."

3 Gardner, V. and Atkinson, D. (n1) pp. 124-5. (Includes all quotations used in this section).

4 Left: www.museumoflondon.org.uk/discover/celebrating-suffragette-courage-london-history-day accessed 22.12.2021
Article celebrating the lives of four suffragettes, including Kitty Marion, written by Beverley Cook, curator of The Museum of London 'Votes for Women' exhibition.
Right: www.npg.org.uk/collections/search/person/mp58993/kitty-marion-katherina-maria-schafer?search=sas&Text=Kitty+Marion accessed 22.12.2021
A group of photographs of Kitty held at The National Portrait Gallery, London.

5 Gardner, V. and Atkinson, D. (n1), pp. 128 - 137.

6 Gardner, V. and Atkinson, D. (n1), pp. 137-8.

7 Gardner, V. and Atkinson, D. (n1), p. 143.

8 By courtesy of the University of Liverpool Library. 0 55/17/2/2 Stanley Jones Special Archives, Liverpool University. Handwritten, the letter has an interesting note in the margin, where Mrs. Solomon refers to the Metropolitan police as "the police force called 'The Hen Catcher.'" The file also contains another letter from a friend who witnessed the event.

9 Gardner, V. and Atkinson, D. (n1), pp. 159 – 163.

10 Working Class Movement Library, Suffrage Boxes, BOX 1, Page 35

11 https://artsandculture.google.com/asset/scrapbook-compiled-by-the-suffragette-kitty-marion-marion-kitty/AQEjloxG7PwDrg?hl=en p 6. Accessed 8.3.22
This is a digitized form of Kitty's scrapbook of press cuttings 1909 – 1916 relating to her part in the militancy campaign. Detailed notes about the events and her annotations accompany the scrapbook.

12 *Wrexham Advertiser*, 5th September 1912, p. 8.

13 https://artsandculture.google.com/asset/scrapbook-compiled-by-the-

suffragette-kitty-marion-marion-kitty/AQEjloxG7PwDrg?hl=en (n11) p7 accessed 8.3.22

14 Gardner, V. and Atkinson, D. (n1), pp. 165-6.

15 https://artsandculture.google.com/asset/note-written-on-prison-toilet-paper-by-kitty-marion/VwFQuzDDIwfi0Q accessed 22.4.22
This is a digital image of Kitty's letter with enclosed hair, accompanied by a full explanation.

16 *Votes for Women*, 13th September 1912, pp. 802-3.

17 Gardner, V. and Atkinson, D. (n1), p. 166.

18 Votes for Women, 13th September 1912, p. 802.

19 DWL 197/17-28, Denbighshire Constabulary Division for Special Services, Wrexham Archives.

20 Gardner, V. and Atkinson, D. (n1), p. 166.

21 *Daily Herald*, 14th October 1912, p. 2.

22 *Anti-suffrage Review*, October 1912, pp. 236-7.

23 *Western Mail*, 6th September 1912, p. 4.

24 *Common Cause*, 19th August 1909, p. 242.

25 *North Wales Guardian*, 21st April 1911, p.5 and 5th May 1911, p.6.

26 *North Wales Guardian*, 30th May1913, p. 8.

27 Wallace R, *The women's suffrage movement in Wales*, University of Wales Press, Cardiff (2018), pp. 84-5

28 *The Suffragette*, 15th August 1913, p. 11.

29 *London Evening Standard*, 11th March 1913, p.9.

30 *Londonderry Sentinel*, 13th March 1913, p.7.

31 *Westminster Gazette*, 16th April 1913, p.11.

32 *Hendon & Finchley Times*, 2nd May 1913. p.5.

33 *Abingdon Free Press*, 2nd May 1913, p.3.

34 Gardner, V. and Atkinson, D. (n1) pp. 170-9.

35 Gardner, V. and Atkinson, D. (n1) pp. 4-5, p.184.

36 www.npg.org.uk/collections/search/portrait/mw194642/Surveillance-Photograph-of-Militant-Suffragettes accessed 11.3.22
Covert surveillance photographs of militant suffragettes to aid with their recognition, held in The National Portrait Gallery.

37 Gardner, V. and Atkinson, D. (n1), pp193 - 7

38 Gardner, V. and Atkinson, D. (n1), pp 207 -219

39 Left: Kitty Marion selling Birth Control Review, www.bl.uk/collection-items/photograph-of-kitty-marion-selling-birth-control-review
Right: Cartoon of Kitty Marion, unknown source. New York Public Library. "Urchin: Aw! Lookit the Statya of Liberty!" The New York Public Library Digital Collections. 1923 - 1927. https://digitalcollections.nypl.org/items/b8838970-fa1b-0135-9983-3b4a80f8de44

40 Bailey A Dickerson, 1926, "A Tribute to Miss Marion", BCR, June 1926, p 200

41 Unattributed, 1918, "Judges with Small Families Jail Kitty Marion," BCR, November 1918, p. 5

42 Gardner, V. and Atkinson, D. (n1) p. 262.

43 Gardner, V. and Atkinson, D. (n1) pp. 236-8.

44 Gardner, V. and Atkinson, D. (n1) p. 252-5.

45 *New Yorker*, 4th July 1936, pp. 22-4.

46 Gardner, V. and Atkinson, D. (n1) pp. 268 – 271.

Appendix

Articles in *Birth Control Review* by Kitty Marion

1921 Scattered Memories, Sept, pp. 11, 14, 15.

1923 Ye that pass by, February, p 45.

1925 The Catholics on the Sidewalk of New York March, p.84 & p.91, and Friends on the street, November, p. 322.

1926 People I meet, Feb, p 69; St Patrick's Day, a note from KM for the RC Laity, May, p 166; A tribute to Kitty Marion, June, p 200; Editorial explaining her arrest, Oct p 297; The people of New York v Miss Kitty Marion. Oct p. 306.

1927 Reflections in the Christmas Crowds of 1926, Feb, p. 55; Catholics, Aug, p229; News Notes, p. 231; Editorial, Kitty Marion's arrest, Sept, p. 236.

1928 A Corner for Kitty Marion, Jan, p. 30; A Few of St Patrick's Paraders, May, p155; Heard on the street, Aug p. 237; Contrasted Views, Dec, p 355.

1930 Hail and Farewell! March, p. 92.

A Better World for Women: Mary Quaile and Women Trade Unionists Visit the Soviet Union in 1925

by Bernadette Hyland

In 2022 it feels like the word *hope* has left the political vocabulary. Politics today seems to be just about trying to hang on to our jobs and our public services. It feels as if we are all in the gutter, not looking at the stars.

In 1925 things were not much better, particularly for women. After the end of the First World War female membership in trade unions declined, and continued to do so throughout the 1920s and 1930s, while unemployment rose and wages fell. Cheap female labour was used by employers to displace men while the trade union movement struggled to attract women because it failed to address their particular needs as workers, carers and citizens.

Many people in Britain looked to the new society being created in the Soviet Union as a blueprint for a better world. In April 1925 a group of British women trade unionists set off on a four month fact-finding visit to the Soviet Union on behalf of the TUC. Mary Quaile chaired the delegation, reflecting her national status in the trade union movement. When Margaret Bondfield was appointed as Parliamentary Secretary to the Minister of Labour in January 1924 in the first Labour Government, Mary had taken her place on the General Council of the TUC.

The women's delegation took place because it was felt that, although a delegation of trade unionists

had visited the Soviet Union the previous year, "the delegation had not included women, who it might be urged would be quick to appreciate conditions affecting the work, health and general conditions of women and children in Russia."

The delegation was made up of four women. In addition to Mary, there was Mrs. A. Bridge, an organiser in the National Union of Printing, Bookbinding and Paper Workers; Miss Annie Loughlin, an organiser in the Tailor and Garment Workers Union; and Miss L. A. Aspinall, an organiser in the Weavers, Winders and Reelers Association. The delegation also included a stenographer, Miss Kay Purcell, and an interpreter, Mrs. Z. Coates. It is hard to imagine today how mindblowing it must have been for these working class women to visit the Soviet Union in an era when foreign travel was usually confined to the middle-class. Just looking at this photo of them leaving shows how excited and happy they look.

The delegation started out in Moscow, and then travelled across the country to Leningrad, Kharkov, the Crimea, Balaclava, Sebastopol, Rostov-on-Don, Kislovodsk, Grozny, Baku,Tiflis, Borzhom, Abas-Timan and Vladikavkaz. They countered criticism that they were being manipulated by the Soviet authorities by stating; "Whilst the local trade union and Soviet Authorities made suggestions, it was the delegation itself who decided where they should go, and what they should see, the authorities always providing all the necessary facilities."

It was not just the geographical breadth of the women's tour that was wide ranging, but the subjects they investigated: factory workshops, social insurance, social issues, national minorities, textile industry, women in industry and other topics. The printed report has some wonderful pictures, not just of factories but of a Tartar Mosque in Georgia, a workers' rest home in the Caucasus, and peasants at a Peasant Congress.

The women delegates were all women who regularly visited local mills and factories in Britain and so were able to comment as experts on the working conditions they saw in the Soviet Union. This is evident in the chapter on the Textile Industry where they looked at the way in which the work was organised compared to British mills, and noticed how much better the working conditions were.

In one of the garment factories they visited they commented that it was run on American lines because of an arrangement between the Russian Garment Makers Trade Union and the Amalgamated Clothing Workers of America, who supplied them with new machinery. The delegates were able to speak to these workers more freely because they were Americans who had come over in 1920.

The Soviet Union was committed in theory to the equality of the sexes, but as the country embarked

Banner given to the delegation by Soviet Women
(TUC collection)

on the New Economic Policy, which reintroduced a measure of privately run business, women were losing their jobs and being relegated to low skill work. The delegates reported that this was being countered by allowing women to work in previously prohibited work, including night work, and by raising the education level of women.

And, whilst in both Britain and the Soviet Union there were debates about how women were going to achieve equality, in the chapter on "The Family in Soviet Russia" the answer was clear: provide communal resources such as public dining rooms and access to social clubs with childcare facilities. They also report on the position of unmarried women with children, marriage and divorce, as well as the mutual rights and duties of parents and children. These were policies well ahead of British attitudes and legislation in the 1920s.

Women's Delegation leaving Victoria

1. G. Hicks
2. A. Conley
3. F. B. Varley, M.P
4. R. Coppick
5. B. Tillett
7. W. Lawther
9. B. Turner
10. A. A. Purcell, M.P.
12. R. Smillie, M.P.
13. Miss M. Purcell
14. Mrs. Z. K. Coates
15. Miss M. Quaile
16. Miss A. Loughlin
17. Mrs. L. A. Aspinall
18. Mrs. A. Bridge

British Trade Union Women's Delegation with Georgian women

Unusual for any delegation at that time was the inclusion of an analysis of organisations specifically for children. The delegates spoke to children in the Young Pioneers, an organisation for children of 11-16 years – comparing with the more militarised British Scout Movement – and could actually speak and report verbatim the views of one of the children.

In 2022 we could and should be sceptical about the rosy views painted by the delegates in this report. But the delegates have no qualms about this as they state in the conclusion that they thought there was enough negative reporting of the Soviet Union, and that they "have emphasised the good because the bad is entirely an inheritance of the past; the good is the work of the present and an earnest hope of the future" and that "no honest observer of present-day Soviet Russia can doubt for one moment that a great and sincere experiment in working class government is being carried out in Russia."

Christine Coates, former librarian at the TUC, kindly alerted me to an article that Mary wrote about her trip in the monthly journal *Trade Union Unity* in August 1925. This journal is available at the Working Class Movement Library.

Our Women's Delegation to Russia by Mary Quaile

The visit to Russia of six British working women is a milestone on the road to international Trade Union unity. It will long live in our memories and also in the memories of the thousands of workers that greeted us wherever we travelled in that great country. We left London on April 23, and were met in Riga by comrades from the Central Council of the Russian Trade Unions, but our first great welcome came when we stopped at the first town across the border from Latvia.

Women were there in hundreds, many of them with bunches of wild flowers to give to their British sisters, all of them wanting to shake our hands, some with tears in their eyes, not of sorrow, but of joy at our meeting. There also came to greet us children, the pioneers of the new social order, which will emancipate the workers of the world. It was Sunday, but these workers in their hundreds had been out early planting their trees to give value and beauty to the country they now owned. This was voluntary work, but it was done in the willing spirit that afterwards we met with so often in Russia.

Moscow was reached a day sooner than was expected, but a tremendous welcome awaited us with bands, banners, flowers and speeches. One was glad and proud to be a member of the class that demonstrated so plainly their love for the women workers of Britain. Our tour of Russia took us to Leningrad, back again to Moscow, down through the Ukraine via Kharkoff,

The delegation in Kislovodsk

and then to the Don Basin, the Crimea, Rostov, Kislovodsk, Grozny, Baku, Tiflis, Borjom, Akhaltsikh, Abastuman and Vladikavkas.

Visits were made to factories, mines, oil wells, rest homes, sanatoria, nurseries and children's hospitals, schools, universities, museums and workers' houses, both old and new. Co-operative stores,peasants' villages,farms for experimental purposes were also investigated by the delegation.

I can best summarise our impressions by paraphrasing the preliminary statement we issued on our return

"After many personal talks with the workers of all trades and grades,including peasants and agricultural workers, we have no hesitation in saying that the Soviet Government not only has the enthusiastic support of the vast majority of the workers and peasants, but that both these classes of workers look upon the present Government as essentially their own. There is certainly a dictatorship in Russia, but it is a workers' and peasants' dictatorship. The Russian Communist Party is undoubtedly the directive force, but it is the workers and peasants through their elected soviets or councils that rule.

Women are encouraged as far as possible to enter all classes of work, and for equal work they receive equal pay. Their entry into industry is facilitated by the fact that most factories have nurseries and kindergartens attached where the women can leave their children to be cared for by skilled attendants, and this in most cases is free of any charge.

In addition to this every month every woman factory worker gets two months leave of absence before and after the birth of her child, with full wages. All sorts of other benefits, such as food and clothing, are provided.

Workers' canteens or communal dining rooms help to make the domestic drudgery very much less for working wife or mother.

The health of the worker is a first charge on industry, and rest homes and sanatoria are a feature of Russian life which will give the workers a better chance to carry on their great work of reconstructing their industries and abolishing many of the evils inherited from the capitalist regime.

The workers showed a very lively interest in the cause of Trade Union unity, as the tremendous May Day demonstrations which we witnessed in Moscow made clear to us. We were asked many questions about the chances of a real international United Front. They see in this movement a chance for the workers of all countries to emancipate themselves from capitalism and also to afford greater protection for the Russian workers from the many machinations of the imperialist Governments of the world.

The British workers have in the past often stood by the Russian workers. Let them once more lead the way in a movement to strengthen and protect the pioneer Worker's Republic. Let us appeal to the leaders of our workers' movement to come together, and with their great organising powers, set themselves the task of understanding and building up the united Trade Union organisation, national and international, that is so necessary to the working class of the world."

Thanks to the Working Class Movement Library.

Mary Quaile at TUC meeting

This is the conclusion of the women's report

IN giving our report of what we saw and learned during our visit to Soviet Russia, we are not at all concerned with the question as to the righteousness of the Bolsheviks, or as to their methods of establishing the Soviet system. In investigating conditions in a foreign country we have to take institutions as we find them, and only two things concern us : firstly, is that system accepted by the majority of the people who live under it ? secondly, does it on the whole work out for the benefit of the toiling masses of the country ? With Mr. Keynes we say quite frankly that we are definitely and all the time on the side of our own class, the exploited working class (including working peasants and both brain and hand workers).

As to the question of whether the Soviet Government is accepted by the people who live under it, we have no hesitation in giving a very emphatic " Yes." The vast majority of the town workers and the more educated of the peasantry in every part of the Soviet Union we visited, are enthusiastically in its favour ; they take a pride in its achievements, and feel that, so far from the Soviet Government being the dictatorship of a comparatively small party, it is the expression of their own dictatorship –the dictatorship of the workers and peasants. They look to the Russian Communist Party for leadership. They respect and love it as the party that has led them to success ; but State power, they feel, is actually under their own control, through their direct representatives on the soviets, through their trade unions, their workshop committees, and so on.

As regards the masses of the illiterate and backward peasantry, they give the Soviet Government at least their passive support. Their life is still very hard, but so it was formerly—who is to blame they do not know ; they do not understand the " high politics " of the townspeople—but most of them do know that they have more land now than formerly. Some of them do appreciate the fact that in time of drought and special hardships the State conies to their help far more frequently and readily than had ever been the case before. More and more of them are beginning to appreciate the efforts being made by the Government and town workers to spread education amongst them and to give them some of the benefits o of modern science, or, as they say themselves, " some of the present-day wonders," such as electricity, agricultural machinery, aerial methods of pest destruction, and so on.

There still remains the intelligentsia, or semi-intelligentsia, and the private employers and traders. The intelligentsia, in so far as they are represented by such classes as teachers, doctors, professors, and journalists, for the most part support the Government, either actively or at the very least passively. We met many of them in schools, hospitals, colleges. and privately, as our report shows. We met some privately who are not active supporters of the Government, who would pmbably acquiesce in another form of government equally well, but what struck us was the way in which they. took the Soviet Government for granted as their own stable Government. They criticised some of the activities of Soviet Government—but not nearly so vehemently as the Government of the day in England may be heard to be criticised any day. Nevertheless, a housewife, for instance, in one ease, showing us her two children (very bonny ones, aged ten and two respectively, who did not look at all as though they had gone through the hard days of the wars, revolution, famine, and blockade) said : " Just look at his little limbs, don't imagine that our soviet children are starved or neglected !

We also spoke to a number of private shopkeepers when they did not know who we were, to hairdressers, and private employers. Here it is quite true that in many cases they complained of various restrictions, inure particularly of the restrictions imposed by the Government in the first years of the Revolution. For the most part, however, they also said that things were improving, and in any case there was no question of regarding the Soviet Government as anything but a permanency, They may not like it, but they certainly realise its strength—that is to say, the support it has from the masses, and they accept it with more acquiescence and far less hope of overthrowing it than Socialists and supporters of the Labour Party in Great Britain accept the present Conservative Government.

We admit that our report deals mainly with the best side of present-day life in Soviet. Russia. We do not at all mean to deny that there is still much suffering, much poverty in the Soviet Union. We are perfectly well aware that the work still awaiting the Soviet. Government in the spheres of education, of raising the general cultural level of the people of that vast country, as in agriculture, industry, housing, sanitation, health, is still enormous. If we have described and emphasised the good, it is for two reasons. In the first place, there are not lacking scribes in this and other countries who are continually, not merely painting the bad sides of present-day Soviet. Russia, but exaggerating them out of all proportion. Secondly, and far more important, we have emphasised the good because the had is entirely an inheritance of the past : the good is the work of the present and an earnest of the hope of the future.

Although in this report we do not desire to discuss the question as to whether the soviet system is applicable or not to this or other countries, we can say that in Russia, at any rate, it has lent itself to a far more genuine and widespread participation of the masses of the workers, and of those working peasants who take an interest in public affairs, in the actual machinery of every-day government, than is the ease here at home. Moreover, it is the constant endeavour of the Soviet authorities. of the Russian Communist Party, and the Russian trade unions, to draw larger and larger sections of the toiling masses, urban and rural, men and women, to participate in the work of government.

Whatever our abstract. theoretical views may be of the soviet system of government, however we may differ from the Bolsheviks in points of detail, or even in general outlook as regards the position of affairs in our own country, no honest observer of present-day Soviet Russia can doubt for one moment that a great and sincere experiment in working-class government is being carried out in Russia. We consider : that this experiment is worthy of the interest, sympathy. and assistance of the workers of the world that there is much in Soviet Russia that our workers might do well study : that so far this experiment has resulted in bringing about enormous benefits for the toiling masses of Russia : that these hem-tits are and are likely to become more and more widespread as thee economic position of the country recovers from the dealt it by the world imperialism and capitalism, and from the ruin and miseries it has inherited from the Tsarist regime.

M. QUAILE
A. BRIDGE
A. LOUGHLIN
L. A. ASPINALL

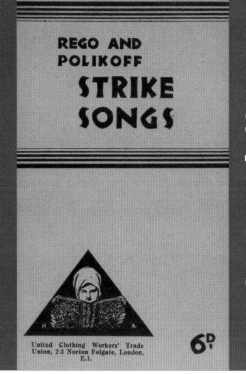

REGO AND
POLIKOFF
STRIKE
SONGS

United Clothing Workers' Trade
Union, 2-3 Norton Folgate, London,
E.1.

6ᴰ

"We are no dirty shirkers…": The Rego and Polikoff Strike Songs

In this article we present a selection from the Rego and Polikoff Strike Songs songbook which featured some 35 songs written by the strikers at these two factories.

In the autumn of 1928 600 young women and a small number of men at the Rego clothing factory went out on strike over piecework payments which escalated into a strike over union recognition. That summer the factory had been moved from Bethnal Green Road, Shoreditch, to new, larger premises in Edmonton. The employer decided that, as the factory was now "outside' of London, they did not have to pay the higher London wages and reduced the women's pay. For a 49-hour week, a girl aged 16 earned around 14 shillings, out of which she had now to pay 4s 6d for fares, which she had not had to pay before because most of the young women lived within walking distance of the old factory, and also 3s 9d for dinners and teas, because they could not go home for dinner any more. They were left with 4s or less per week to hand over to their mothers for keep.

Rego also introduced a conveyor belt system, which meant that everyone had to work at the same speed with no bonuses for quicker workers. Then one woman refused to pay her union dues and was encouraged in this by the management. The rest of

the unionised women demanded that she either pay her union subscriptions, or be sacked. When the management refused this, a strike began on 8th October. The vast majority of the strikers were women, some only about 15 or 16 years old.

One of strike leaders by Sarah Wesker (1901- 1971) who grew up in the East End Jewish community, spoke Yiddish as well as English, and had been active in a number of strikes by garment workers eg in 1926 she had led a strike for more pay at Goodman's trouser factory.

The strike was supported by the London District of the Tailors' and Garment Workers' Union, but not by the Executive, which meant that the strikers received no money from their own union, to which, of course, they had been contributing their weekly dues. The union's London organiser was Sam Elsbury, who, by contrast, fully supported the strike. Sam was a naturalised British citizen who had emigrated from Russia; his original name was Solomon Elfski. He was an active member of the Communist Party of Great Britain, formed in 1920, and also the Minority Movement, established by the Communist party in 1924 to organise a rank-and-file movement in trade unions in opposition to union leaderships. Its President was the veteran trade unionist, Tom Mann.

THE REGO CLOTHIERS LTD.

MANUFACTURING CLOTHIERS.
UNIFORMS & EQUIPMENTS

CONTRACTORS TO
H. M. GOVERNMENT

CHIEF OFFICES WAREHOUSES & FACTORY
ESTABLISHED 1874

ANGEL ROAD,
EDMONTON,
LONDON, N.18.

BRANCHES THROUGHOUT
LONDON & HOME COUNTIES

Telephone
TOTTENHAM 270 (5 LINES)
Telegrams
REGOCLO, TOTTLE, LONDON
Cables
A B C CODE 5TH EDITION

TE/EH.

April 17th. 1937.

Rego letterhead

As they were not receiving any strike pay, the women raised money by singing songs they had written to the tunes of popular songs of the day and went out collecting. In mid October they were allowed by Tottenham Hotspur FC to collect at the match between Spurs and London Caledonians.

The collections were successful. On 24th October, for instance, the *Daily Herald* reported that a second payout of £500 a week had been made, although it was not distributed evenly but by sex ; the men received a £1, but the women only got 10 shillings, presumably because it was thought that the men had families to support. The notion of "a family wage" for men persisted among many trade unionists up until the 1970s, when the Equal Pay Act was brought in.

The women organised mass pickets at the factory and also picketed the 80 odd retail shops owned by the firm. They also attended marches and rallies eg in November they marched to a rally in Trafalgar Square organised by the International Class War Prisoners' Aid. The women received some support from other unions: the Electrical Trade Union told the Rego management that, even though the strike was not recognised by the TGWU, they believed that "the object of the strike was is thoroughly justified, and that, the object being to gain better conditions and full recognition, it is their bounden duty to render the strikers support"; the London Trades Council also affirmed its support in early December; while the miners' leader, A J Cook, was one of the speakers at rally in Edmonton in November.

According to the *Daily Herald*, the example of the strike at Rego led women at the nearby Lissen wireless factory to ask for more money – which the firm immediately conceded.

At the end of November the company served writs against Sam Elsbury, Bernard Sullivan (the London District secretary) and the Tailors and Garment Workers' Union, alleging a conspiracy to "induce breach of contracts." It also sought to restrain the defendants from alleged "intimidation and from publishing or circulating pamphlets or documents containing libellous suggestions or suggestions calculated to injure the firm's trade."

The strike was successful and ended on 21st December, just in time for Christmas. At a hearing regarding the writs held in January 1929 the counsel for Rego, Mr Spens, KC, told the judge that all matters in dispute had been cleared up and work had resumed. Both sides would pay their own costs while the company would pay the costs of the union.

In March the *Daily Herald* reported that Executive of the Tailors' Union had dismissed Sam from his post "having examined correspondence and other written matter in connection with the Rego dispute particularly, and certain aspects of the administration of London branch business. The Board declared that, in its opinion, Mr Elsbury acted contrary to the decision of the Executive Board in reference to the Rego strike and had continued that policy up to date. Mr. Elsbury has been an official of the union since April, 1919.

A meeting of London members was held the next day and this led to the formation of a breakaway union, the United Clothing Workers' Union, with Sam as the General Secretary. Sarah Wesker was on the Executive and later became the women's organiser. Later that year there was a strike for union recognition by UCWU members at Polikoff's factory who also used songs for fund-raising. However, unlike at Rego's, this strike ended in defeat.

Though initially successful in attracting most of Tailor's Union members in London, the UCWU only lasted until 1935 due to financial difficulties and the hostility of the Tailors' Union who put pressure on employers not to recognise the UCWU. Its members then re-joined the Tailors' Union, including Sarah Wesker who surprisingly perhaps, was elected on to the Executive and worked to organise women into the union. In 1932 she was elected onto the Central committee of the Communist party.

In October 1936 Sarah took part in the Battle of Cable Street in which tens of thousands of East Enders successfully defeated an attempt by the Metropolitan Police to violently force a fascist march through the East End. Her nephew was the playwright Arnold Wesker who, in his play *Chicken Soup With Barley* (1958), based the character of Cissie Kahn (describing her as "precise in her manner, dry sense of humour") on his aunt. In this extract Cissie describes what happened at Cable Street:

Cissie. Some of the boys from my union got arrested.

Sarah. I'll go and make some tea now.

Cissie. Mick and Sammy and Dave Goldman — and that bloody fool, if you'll excuse the expression, Sonny Becks.

Everybody is standing behind the barricades waiting for the blackshirts to appear. The place is swarming with policemen waiting, just waiting, for an opportunity to lay their hands on some of us. So look what he does: not content with just standing there — and Sonny knew perfectly well that the orders were for the strictest discipline — not content with just standing he chose that moment to get up on Mrs O'Laoghaire's vegetable barrow and make a political speech. 'Let us now remember the lessons of the Russian revolution,' he starts like he was quoting Genesis, the nitwit.

And then he finds that the barrow isn't safe so he steps over to an iron bedstead and put his foot through the springs just as he was quoting Lenin's letter to the toiling masses!

Monty. You can never stop Sonny making a speech.

Cissie. But not in bed ! Anyway, you know Sonny — a mouth like a cesspool and no shame — so he lets out a torrent of abuse at the capitalist bed-makers and the police just make a dive at him. Mick and Sammy tried to argue with the police so they were hauled off and then Dave Goldman tried to explain — that was when he was hauled off, poor bastard, if you'll excuse the expression !

Hymie. What'll happen ?

Cissie. The union'll have to find the lawyers and probably pay their fine — what else ? Which reminds me — Monty and Prince. Get all the boys and girls you can find and bring them to that social next Saturday, the one for Sally Oaks.

Hymie. Wasn't it her husband caught his bicycle in a tram-line and was killed?

Cissie. That's right. She's a Catholic. The local priest is trying to raise some money to keep her going for a bit and we promised we'd support it. Well, I'm going.

In 1929 the United Clothing Workers' Union published the songs in a booklet. In his foreword Sam Elsbury wrote:

These strike songs are ditties developed during

HE WHO WAS OBEYED !
(Acknowledgements to "The Young Worker")

two great struggles of the London clothing workers. The use of this type of strike song is a new feature in British working class history and is on to be seriously reckoned with as a weapon in future activity.

When the Rego strike broke out, that of 600 workers, mostly poorly paid girls, against attacks on their already low living standards, trade unionists shook their heads and predicted an early defeat. Most of the girls were completely without previous experience of trade unionism and the fact that their strike was not only refused endorsement by their union's National Executive in Leeds, but was definitely attacked by it, made defeat tenfold certain. As an "unofficial "strike no union funds were, of course, available for strike pay, and the outlook for the strike was, therefore, about as bad as it conceivably could be. Nevertheless, this apparently hopeless lasted 12 weeks and terminated as Xmas, 1928, with the victory of the strikers.

It is common knowledge how the Rego strikers were supported. Workers and working class bodies and sympathisers came gallantly to the aid of the plucky strikers from all parts of the country and even of the world. Russian needle workers, for instance, sent one contribution of £216 to the aid of these British fellow workers.

But, more important even than funds in such a strike was the maintenance of morale of the strikers and it was the high standard of this which enlisted the great support given in the strike and ensured its eventual success. Here it was that the Strike Songs played such an important part. The strikers marched frequently to all parts of London to obtain and became known as "The Singing Strikers" for reason of their extensive use of their Strike Songs.

By the end of the strike their repertoire of these songs was extensive and it might almost be said that, combined with their militant leadership, the strikers *sang* themselves into victory.

We have space only for a few of these songs which, unpolished as several of them are, breathe such a fine proletarian spirit that they are worthy of being preserved for the benefit of other workers. Their authorship is not acknowledged for several reasons. That of many of the songs is not known. Others of the songs were written co-operatively; several hands participating in the constructing of each. For these and for other reasons no names of the writers are attached to the songs

It is not surprising that this weapon of the Rego strikers should be taken up by the Polikoff strike which commenced in May, 1929. The causes of this strike require some explanation in order to appreciate the songs written upon it.

As a direct result of the Rego strike the Executive of the Tailors' and Garment Workers' Union were approached by the Clothing Employers' Federation to discipline their London militant officials if "amicable relations" between them were to continue. In March, 1929, the Executive effected this discipline by dismissing Sam Elsbury, their London organiser.

The London branch's reply was to break away from the boss controlled union and to set up the United Clothing Workers' Union of which Sam Elsbury is the General Secretary.

Polikoff, one of the largest London Clothing employers and a member of his Federation, refused to continue "recognition" to the new union and attempted to get his employees back into the fold of the T and G.W.U. 700 of the employees struck, after much provocation, for

Front cover of fashion magazine published by Rego

the "recognition" of their union, the UCWU, those who remained at work ("blacklegs") being immediately enrolled into the T and G.W.U which actually acted as a strikebreaking agency for the firm during the entire course of the strike.

In this unprecedented struggle it will be seen, therefore, that the strikers were faced not only by the employer and his Federation, but also by the T. and G.W.U. and the Trades Union Congress General Council on which this "union" has a representative in the person of A. Conley, its General Secretary. Attacked on all these fronts, the strikers put up a splendid fight against the "Mondist" combination of employers and union "leaders" but were at last compelled to temporarily give way to the tremendous pressure exerted on them. Although they returned to work, all of them pledged themselves to remain loyal to the union that refused to be "part and parcel" of the capitalist machine for extracting profits for the boss.

Their songs manifest the splendid attitude of the 700 strikers during the course of the dispute. As the strength of the clothing workers increases at the expense of the reactionaries, a complete victory will undoubtedly be secured in the near future.

The Cable Street Mural in the East End of London, painted by Dave Binnington Savage, Paul Butler, Ray Walker and Desmond Rochfort.

The Rego Strikers!

(Tune: Donkey Row Lads)

We are the Rego Strikers!
We are no dirty shirkers!
We know our manners,
Behind our Union banners,
We want Justice wherever we go,
When we went to Edmonton,
They thought they had us whacked!
But we know we're in the right,
And we're sure to win the fight,
We are the Rego girls!
(This song, sung with defiant determination, was always the one which led off the Rego Strike Songs in the Strikers' Marches.)

The Rego Girls

(Tune: Mary had a little lamb)

The Rego Girls are marching with spirits all aglow,
Shouting out the battle cry of freedom
And everywhere that Elsbury went the girls were sure to go,
Shouting out the battle cry of freedom,
Harrah for Elsbury! Never mind the "Daves"
Harrah for the Rego girls who won't be slaves,
And everywhere that Elsbury went the girls were sure to go,
Shouting out the battle cry of freedom
Hurrah, hurrah, hurrah, hurrah
Wizz bang, wizz bang, wizz bang. Rah!
Who the hell d'ye think we are?

STRIKERS!

We're Not Down-Hearted

(Tune: Brokenhearted)
We stand up for our right,
And we mean to win this fight
That is why we're not downhearted!
They may say what they like –
We know why we're out on strike!
So let them know we're downhearted.
When they hit below the belt
They thought they knocked us out.
But we hit back, and what they felt
Was enough to make them shout -"Oh"
Here We go. Hear our song
We shall win. It won't take long
And that is why we're not down-hearted !

The "Daily Herald"

(Tune: London bridge is falling down)

The "Daily Herald" is no good
Is no good, is no good.
The "Daily Herald" is no good,
Oh, what a Labour paper.
The T.G.W is no good,
Is no good, is no good
The T.G.W is no good,
The bosses bought them over.
Polikoff's strikers they are good
They are good, they are good,
Polikoff's strikers they are good;
They can't buy them over!

Solidarity for Ever

(Tune: John Brown's Body)

When the Union's aspiration through the Polikoff
workers run,
There can be no power greater anywhere beneath the
sun,
Yet what force on earth is weaker than the feeble
strength of one?
But the Union makes us strong
Solidarity for ever
Solidarity for ever
Solidarity for ever
But the union makes us strong
We will all support our leaders, who are going to pull us
through,
They are not the type of Conley and all his dirty crew,
We'll get victory in this battle, we are many, they are few
For the Union makes us strong
Solidarity for ever
Solidarity for ever
Solidarity for ever

Mare Street Hackney

(Tune: Tipperary)

Out in Mare Street, Hackney, there's a shop that we all
know,
It's a firm that has the habit of making lots of "dough",
The workers said, "We want our share!" At which the
boss did scoff.
You can guess the kind employer's name, t'was Mr.
Polikoff
It's a long way to fight for freedom,
It's a long way to go,
It's strong way to fight for freedom,
And we'll get there some day, you know
Good-bye, Alfred Polikoff!
Good-bye slavery!
It's a long way to fight for freedom,
But we'll get there, that's so!
The boss told all his workers, "Join the union I like"
But they replied, "We'll see you (h'm) and they went out
on strike.
A union they wanted, not a goose club for the boss.
"The Clothing Workers' Union is the one for us, Old
Hoss!"
It's a long way to fight for freedom,
It's a long way to go,
It's strong way to fight for freedom,
And we'll get there some day, you know
Good-bye, Alfred Polikoff!
Good-bye slavery!
It's a long way to fight for freedom,
But we'll get there, that's so!

So that is why we're striking and the boss has got a
pain,
From toe nails to his cranium it's sending him insane.
His union of scabs and him can call all profits "off!"
Until he throws the sponge up. Do ye hear that, Polikoff?
It's a long way to fight for freedom,
It's a long way to go,
It's strong way to fight for freedom,
And we'll get there some day, you know
Good-bye, Alfred Polikoff!
Good-bye slavery!
It's a long way to fight for freedom,
But we'll get there, that's so!

The Union Banner

(Tune: Bandiera Rossa)

We work at Polikoff's
All factory workers,
United under the Union Banner
We raise our emblems
To all the blacklegs
The union banner triumphantly
Raise the Union Banner triumphantly
Raise the Union Banner triumphantly
Raise the Union Banner triumphantly
For recognition and liberty!
For our employers
We built up profits
From all out toiling,
It was our blunder,
We now march under
Our Union Banner triumphantly
Raise the Union Banner triumphantly
Raise the Union Banner triumphantly
Raise the Union Banner triumphantly
For recognition and liberty!
When this strike's over
We will remember
Our fighting Union;
We'll ne'er surrender,
And to the last fight
We'll still match under
Our Union Banner triumphantly.
Raise the Union Banner triumphantly
Raise the Union Banner triumphantly
Raise the Union Banner triumphantly
For recognition and liberty!

Women on the March

Equal Rights Procession, 3rd July 1926

In 1918, after sixty years of campaigning, women finally vote in parliamentary elections, although to begin with only women over 30 were allowed to vote: women finally got the vote on the same terms as men in 1928.

In 1919 Parliament passed the Sex Disqualification (Removal) Act which stated that people should not be disqualified "by sex or marriage from the exercise of any public function, or from being appointed to or holding any civil or judicial office or post, or from entering or assuming or carrying on any civil profession or vocation." This Act (which has often been overlooked) allowed women to serve as magistrates or jurors or enter the professions such the law leading to a small number of women becoming barristers or solicitors. However it did not bring about equal pay or prevent discrimination in employment: women teachers who got married were often sacked by local authorities for instance.

Thus in the 1920s a number of organisations campaigned for further equality in employment, maternity, pay etc. These included the National Union of Societies for Equal Citizenship (formerly the National Union of Women Suffrage Societies), the Six Points Group, the Open Door Council and the Women's Freedom League.

These organisations conducted their campaigns through the traditional constitutional means of public meetings, annual conferences, issuing pamphlets and reports, sending deputations to

Helena Normanton, the first woman barrister

ministers and writing letters to the press. However there was a poignant return to the heady days of suffrage protests when they organised an Equal Rights Procession in London on 3rd July 1926.

The procession followed the traditional route from the Embankment to Hyde Park. where they were numerous platforms with speakers. This report (dated 9th July 1926) is from *The Vote,* the newspaper of the Women's Freedom League.

Some 3,500 women, representing over 40 Societies, lined up on the Embankment, near Charing Cross Bridge, last Saturday afternoon, and walked in procession to Hyde Park, there, with the crowds already assembled, to hold a great mass Demonstration, demanding an immediate Government measure giving votes to women at 21 on the same terms as men, and for Peeresses in their own right a seat, voice, and vote in the House of Lords.

The Procession formed a pageant of beauty and colour as it gathered near the Temple Station, extending finally right across to the Royal Air Force Memorial near the Houses of Parliament. All the colours of the rainbow were reflected in the banners and scrolls and waving pennants of the various Societies participating, amongst which the green, white and gold of the Women's Freedom League contingent (under the splendid marshalling of Miss E. Berry) made a gallant show. Precisely at 2.45 p.m. this mass of moving colour marched slowly up Northumberland Avenue to the tune of " The Marseillaise."

First in order came the Youth Groups, picturesquely clad, and a group of the voteless " Under Thirties." Directly behind walked various political and Suffrage Societies, both British and American, including a contingent of women M.P.s (one of whom, Miss Ellen Wilkinson, had travelled all night in order to walk in the Procession), ex-women M.P.s (including Mrs. Wintringham), and Parliamentary candidates, preceded by a " Big Ben " banner in black on a red ground, whilst women Councillors, Mayors, and Justices of the Peace brought up the rear of this important little group.

Further down the line the Actresses' contingent, under the patronage of Miss Ellen Terry and Miss Lillah McCarthy, robed in green and pink, with decorated lorries, formed a picturesque group, and were followed by women professors, medical women, and students of all types in academic dress, attached to various specialised Societies

represented by each group. Many veterans of earlier days, including Mrs. Despard, Dame Millicent Fawcett, Mrs. Pankhurst, and Dr. Annie Besant, accompanied old friends and comrades. The organised women teachers brought a splendid contingent, with branch banners and decorated cars, allegorical devices and mottoes.

Our own contingent, headed by our band and the League banner, led by Mrs. Despard, who walked all the way with Mrs. Pethick-Lawrence and Dr. Knight, followed by the members of the National Executive Committee and speakers, and ending with our decorated brake, was an impressive part of the long line. Our branches and members rallied to the flag. Portsmouth came up in its own brake full of enthusiastic members. Representatives came from Swansea and other parts, and - many new and old friends joined us to work towards the victory for which we strive.

Great interest was shown in the procession by the general public, ' of whom the majority were men. Many of these last clapped vigorously, not a few raised hats in respectful silence, whilst one bon vivant, watching from behind the plate glass windows of a Pall Mall Club, kissed his hand to the women marchers. He probably received the shock of his life when he caught sight of Lord Balfour of Burleigh, who walked with the women the whole of the way. VOTES and literature sold freely as the Procession went along, and surely there could not have been a single taxi-driver in London who was minus a programme of the events of the day.

Near Hyde Park Corner we were greeted by Miss Alix Clark from a waiting car. Arrived in Hyde Park, the Procession broke up into groups round the 15 platforms awaiting them, and where large crowds were already assembled. At No. 5, the Women's Freedom League Platform, Miss Anna Munro presided, and, after reading the resolutions, which later in the afternoon were carried with acclamation, she explained that the present Demonstration was only the commencement of a tremendous campaign throughout the country for Equal Franchise. Various speakers then put forward their cause. Miss Godwin, one of the "Under Thirties" stoutly denied that the younger women did not want the vote, as had been frequently asserted. The women under 30 were not asking for favours, but for their just rights. Mrs. Nevinson championed the cause of the professional woman under 30, who had not only qualified for

a profession, but was frequently married as well, with husband, children, and home to manage. As the law stood at present, only one woman in fifteen was enfranchised.

Mrs. Pethick-Lawrence described the great political campaign in the coming autumn, of which to-day's Demonstration was inauguratory, and enumerated some of the achievements— legislative and otherwise that women had accomplished since their partial enfranchisement. Alice Park (of the United States) recalled how some American women voted as far back as 1869, but to-day every woman in the United States was enfranchised on the same terms as men. With the exception of Great Britain, no other country in the world made its women wait to become voters until they were 30 years of age. Great Britain to-day was at the tail end of the procession.

Mrs. Zang will asked what was the mysterious change which overtook a woman between the last day of her 29th birthday and the dawn of her 30th, thus making her eligible for political enfranchisement. She appealed to all the younger women present to keep faith with the lads who laid down their lives in the Great War for the cause of Freedom and Justice. Where women remained voteless, these were but empty words.

Mrs. Mustard referred to the recent debate in the House of Lords on the admission of Peeresses, and maintained that it did far more

harm to the Lords than to the women of whom they spoke. The antiquated views and colossal ignorance revealed by the discussion were merely hastening the end of the Upper House.

Mrs. Whetton told the crowd how 13 members of the Portsmouth Branch of the Women's Freedom League had travelled specially to London that day to help forward the cause of the younger women.

Mrs. Flowers referred to suffrage tactics of former days, and said men had not forgotten them. Women of all ages and classes were needed to use their votes and send worthy Members of Parliament of both sexes to the House of Commons. When Mrs. Despard rose to speak, at the close of the afternoon, the crowd broke out spontaneously into the refra'n, " For she's a jolly good fellow." Later, when she could make herself heard, Mrs. Despard begged earnestly for enthusiastic helpers of both sexes, with vision, to further the cause of full freedom in the world.

The Women's March 1928.

In March 1928 the Communist Party of Great Britain organised a march by women in London with contingents joining from different parts of the country. It received little or no coverage in the press. Below we reproduce the pamphlet issued by the Communist party with an account of the march and a number of pictures. (Please note that It contains out-dated racial stereotypes)

THE
MARCH OF THE
WOMEN

TWOPENCE

THE MARCH OF THE
WOMEN

The Communist Party of Great Britain,
16 King Street, Covent Garden, W.C.2

INTRODUCTION

International Women's Day

INTERNATIONAL Women's Day, 1928, stands out as a landmark in the history of British working women. For the first time in their lives, many women broke away from the traditions that in the past had chained them in silent, submissive slavery to the factory or the drudgery of poverty-stricken homes, and came out in the streets to protest against the infamous conditions inflicted on them and their children by British. capitalism.

Three hundred of them travelled from Yorkshire, Lancashire, Notts, Durham and South Wales, under conditions of extreme discomfort, and at the cost of tremendous sacrifice in order to register that protest in London—the heart of the Empire and the seat of the capitalist Government.

Real working-class unity and a living spirit of comradeship were exhibited by the London women, who had worked for three weeks beforehand, preparing a welcome for women they had never seen before, raising money for food and to assist with fares, opening their homes and their hearts to strange women for the simple reason that they were fellow working women, engaged in the same grim struggle as themselves against the capitalist class.

This was comradeship made real, and unity of the working-class no longer a mere slogan but a living, warm and human thing.

No wonder that the women from the provinces were overcome by the welcome they received. Some of them had been waging a bitter struggle almost alone in stark mining villages among the black hills, or in the hard life of the textile areas. In London they found themselves surrounded by a circle of friends, admired and encouraged, marching with light hearts to the music of hands-no longer individuals battling alone, but honourable members of the great army of workers marching towards the emancipation of the toilers of the earth.

It is fitting that a souvenir of such an event should be in existence-, and this is one of the reasons why this little booklet is published. It is also necessary that an event of such historical importance as International Women's Day, 1928, and the details of its organisation should be placed on record as a guide.

It was a genuine movement of the rank and file women members of the Labour Party, Co-operative Guilds, and even of unorganised women, towards class unity under the leadership of the Communist Party. Leaders of the official Labour movement tried to sabot-age the demonstration, either by ignoring it, or, as was done by the " Daily Herald," definitely attempting to prevent knowledge of it reaching the masses of women, by refusing paid advertisements of conferences called for the purpose of organising the demonstration.

In spite of sabotage, the demonstration was an enormous success, and this little pamphlet, with its pictures, will help to fasten in the minds of the women who took part in it, the memory of that wonderful day.

In Scotland, too, although a regular blizzard was blowing and the snow lay a foot deep on the roads, while in Glasgow the magistrates had banned the demonstration, the women turned up in amazingly large numbers—marching or coming by 'bus from all the outlying villages into Glasgow, Bothwell, Lochgelly, Stirling and Camelon where the meetings were held.

Speakers from every quarter testify to the enthusiasm, determination and, fighting spirit which characterised the day's proceedings both in England and Scotland. It is a tribute to the sagacity and clear-sightedness of the Communist Party and to its organising ability that it is the first party in Britain to give organised expression to the desire of working women for a class-conscious participation in the battles of their class, testifying to its declaration that only under the banner of the Communist Party can working class emancipation be achieved.

BETH TURNER,
(National Women's Organiser, Communist Party of Great Britain.)

THE MARCH OF THE WOMEN

WHAT INTERNATIONAL WOMEN'S DAY MEANS

WHAT is one day chosen out of all others as the day on which women the world over celebrate their emergence as a force, fighting not merely for sex freedom, but for class freedom ?

To answer this question, one must go back to the early days of the year 1917. The world was wallowing in the blood-bath of the Great War, and the workers everywhere in the belligerent countries were being sacrificed to the lust of capitalism.

In Russia, the women standing in queues for hours in the bitter black frost of a Russian winter, waiting for the small portion of black bread, passed from mouth to mouth wild rumours of what was happening at the front.

Soon, bread became even more difficult to get, and confirmation of the rumours was brought by soldiers who had deserted from the front. The men in the trenches were starving. They were without boots and clothing, guns or ammunition, and were being sent against the enemy to fight with sticks or their bare fists.

The women became desperate. Their loved ones at the front were being slaughtered, and their babies at home were dying of starvation. They themselves were haggard and lean with the hunger that gnawed at their very vitals.

Their rage and resentment overleaped all bounds. On March 8th, 1917, they surged out on to the streets of Petrograd, crying insistently for Bread and Peace. Out of the factories and the homes they drew an ever-increasing army of women. Soldiers were sent out against them, but meeting them on the streets, realising the justice of the demands and the indomitable courage of the women who made them and were prepared to fight for them, they refused to fire and joined the ranks of the revolutionary women.

This marked the beginning of the Bolshevik revolution—the revolution that has given to Russian women liberty and rights such as are possessed by women in no other country in the world.

The Bolshevik revolution was the victory of the working class over capitalism. Because that day marked the entry of working women into the revolutionary struggle of their class, it has been set apart ever since as the one on which revolutionary women all over the world celebrate the heroic actions of the Petrograd women, and rally their working-class sisters to prepare for a world victory of the workers over capitalism.

WHY THE WOMEN ANSWERED

Starvation in the coalfields, cuts in relief, reduction of unemployment benefit for women, a monstrously high maternal mortality, startling increase in the infant death rate, particularly in the mining areas, evictions, unemployment and attacks on textile workers—these were the conditions facing the workers of Britain in March, 1928. On women especially the burden had fallen with frightful force. Women in mining villages, not knowing where the next meal was coming from, wrestled with the ravages of smallpox, brought on by poverty and starvation. One hundred and forty-seven out of every thousand babies born in Chester-le-Street die before they reach the age of one year. This the Medical Officer of Health puts down to the effect of the relief cuts, as mothers were so emaciated by starvation that there was no milk in their breasts for their babies.

The Mines Eight-Hours Act had reduced women's as well as men's lives to slavery. In the mining villages some women with three men in the house on different shifts never got one complete night's rest a week. The fire must be kept going and the pot boiling night and day for meals and baths. These facts working women told in our paper the "Working Woman."

Miner's wives sent their husband's and son's pay tickets to the " Working Woman," and the sums earned ranged from 3s. 9d. to 24 or 25 shillings. In some instances even, the men were left with a debt owing to the company after deductions for rent, back-rent, etc. had been made. Debts incurred during the lock-out began to press more insistently; many pits closed down altogether ; reductions were imposed in Durham and Northumberland, and a fight developed at the Welbeck Colliery, Mansfield, over the question of the owners compelling the men to join the scab union or lose their jobs.

In the Lancashire and textile area (including part of Cheshire) cotton mills were working three days a week, and in some instances had closed down altogether. Two hundred mills were in the hands of the banks, collapsing under the burden of over-capitalisation, and ruin threatened the industry, so the owners say.. A demand was made by the millowners for a reduction in wages of 12½ per cent. and an increase in hours. Scarcely had the clamour caused by this demand subsided when one firm at Stalybridge posted notices demanding a 55½ hour week.

Everywhere, attacks were coming from the employers, but the Labour Party and trade union leaders made no pretence of organising for a fight, but met the employers in Industrial Peace Conferences, talked about the General Election, and displayed energy only in the driving out of Communists and Left-wingers from the movement. Labour Party leaders had signed the Blanesburgh Report, whose provisions reducing the unemployment benefit of women from 15s. to 8s. a week were to become operative in April, 1928. British soldiers had opened fire on Chinese workers, and signs of preparation for war with Soviet Russia were evident.

Such were the day to day descriptions of the lives of the workers and the actions of Labour leaders when a number of women delegates to the celebration of the workers' revolution in Russia returned full of enthusiasm for the benefits and freedom enjoyed by women under workers' rule, and told the women workers what they had seen and heard. It is therefore not surprising that when the Communist Party of Great Britain issued its call to women workers to protest against capitalism, it should meet with so ready a response. The women were waiting for a lead, and when it came they were willing and anxious to follow it.

SO THIS IS LONDON !

On Sunday morning, March 11th, 1928, a party of women were walking along Whitehall. They spoke with a Yorkshire accent, and passed pawky comments on the things they saw.

One young woman broke away from the party at Downing Street, and gave a resounding knock on the door of Mr. Baldwin at No. 10. She didn't wait for an answer. "It was just to let him know we're here," she explained.

Soon all London knew "they were here." They had been pouring into the grey stations of the metropolis from four and six o'clock in the morning. At six London's quiet squares were startled by the sound of laughter and singing, and the clatter of clogs on the pavement. Solitary policemen stared disapprovingly, their evident disgust being greeted with derisive remarks. Bonny young girls in clogs and shawls, too young as yet to bear the brand of weariness and over-work that capitalism stamps on its older victims—older women with faces ravaged by want and thankless toil, yet whose eyes were lit with unconquerable optimism. From the factory, from the wash-tub, from the little homes in smoky towns, kept clean only with the most persistent labour, these women invaded London, determined to let Baldwin and the class he represents "know they were here."

Some set off for Petticoat Lane. Many of the women had never been in London before, and a journey on the Underground was a thrilling adventure. There were wild shrieks of amusement and terror as each one placed a first venturesome foot on the escalator (moving staircase). The spectacle of some, who wished to return the way they had come, trying to walk down an escalator that was moving upward, left the rest of the party and the station staff limp with laughter.

Never was a happier party. The passages of the Underground resounded with laughter, and what a job it was counting the party after every train journey or every trip up or down in the lift !

At last Aldgate was reached. Emerging from the station, everybody looked with eager curiosity on the spectacle of London's East End on a Sunday morning.

SEEING THE SIGHTS

Petticoat Lane. The most cosmopolitan proletarian thoroughfare in the world. Here workers from all corners of the earth jostle each other. Jews from Leeds, Palestine, Russia and Bacon Lane display their wares and employ a persuasive tongue in extolling the inimitable value they are offering for a paltry few pence. British sailors, home on leave, swing along with their rolling, easy gait through the narrow Lane. Lascars with slippered feet, slant-eyed Chinamen, woolly-haired African negroes, young bloods from the Bethnal Green

Road, in wonderful suites of helio, brown and vivid blue, all meet and merge in the stream of humanity flowing through the Lane.

Lively young City waitresses come in flocks chirruping noisily like a lot of sparrows, eating hokey-pokey, sampling the green gherkins displayed outside some of the shops, and purchasing stockings marked "pure silk" at a shilling a pair. The sheen of these same stockings is calculated later on in the day to catch the eye of the young bloods in bright attire, or even of the tall, superior-looking young Guardsmen, who walk about in pairs gazing down on the swarming humans below their great height, with condescending aloofness.

Everything offered is "dirt cheap," from pearl necklaces at sixpence to fur coats at forty guineas. But the women from Yorkshire defy even a Jew to sell them anything they don't require or consider a good bargain, and they arrive again at Aldgate, boasting that in spite of the Lane's tawdry temptations, they have not made a single purchase. But they have seen the East End, and are not impressed, either by the look of it or as one of them said, by "the smell of it."

They recognised too clearly the signs of pinched poverty and want on the people's faces, they saw the mean streets and dingy hovels where London's workers are herded, and their contempt and hatred for capitalism increased.

THE WEST END

From the East to the West of London. From squalid, teeming streets to graceful buildings, spacious thoroughfares, and open spaces. It is a matter of minutes where London's Underground is concerned.

Once again we emerged from the bowels of the earth, but this time we found ourselves on the Embankment. On one side the palatial Savoy Hotel, with its millionaire suites and luxurious appointments, and on the other side the silent Thames, and on one of the seats overlooking it a homeless old man who has spent the night there.

No detail was lost by the observant visitors, and considerable interest was evinced in Scotland Yard, which called forth reminiscences of Sir Basil Thompson and also of the imprisonment suffered by women during the suffrage agitation and the General Strike.

From Scotland Yard to the Houses of Parliament was not very far, and members of the Mother of Parliaments would not have been flattered had they heard the comments of some of the women whose votes they hope to win at the next election.

Westminster Abbey, with its unknown soldier's grave, Whitehall with its Cenotaph and War Museum brought back memories of the war years. At Downing Street some of the women recalled the time when it was barricaded to keep out angry women, and prophesied that the time was not far distant when it would need barricading again against women fighting not for sex but for class freedom.

The changing of the guard caused some amusement, and embarrassing remarks were addressed in broad Yorkshire to the sentries on horseback, who blushed scarlet in their effort to pretend they had not heard them.

After a glimpse at St. James' Palace a tired and hungry party made their way back to a restaurant at King's Cross for dinner.

One exciting moment came when the whole crowd squeezed in the lift at the Tube station, and were in imminent danger of being hurled into the lower regions, minus guide or tickets. Forty-five women at a time was rather too much for the lift attendant, whose nerves were almost shattered by the commotion raised when he attempted to close the gates. The comrade who had been purchasing the tickets dashed up breathlessly and slipped between the closing gates. She held out a handful of tickets. "I've got them," she gasped. ``You can keep 'em !" replied the man sourly. But he didn't mean the tickets.

THE TRAFALGAR SQUARE DEMONSTRATION

International Women's Day, March 11th, 1928, registers the first attempt of the Communist Party to rally together, not only locally but nationally, masses of women from factories, mills, minefields and working-class homes, demonstrating under the banner of the Communist Party their disgust at their appalling plight under capitalism, and their solidarity with working women of all countries.

It was an outstandingly successful attempt in every way. Despite most adverse weather conditions, 5,000 people rallied in Trafalgar Square, the great majority of whom had marched in local contingents from North, South, East and West London to the Embankment and thence to the Square, led by the newly-formed Women's Unit of the Labour League of Ex-Service Men, together with a large contingent of L.L.X. men, who afterwards stewarded the demonstration and guarded the plinth.

Never in the long history of Trafalgar Square demonstrations has there been such a blaze of colour. Red, red, red, wherever the eye rested— banners, posters, slogans, kerchiefs, rosettes, streamers, tableaux. Mill-girls from Lancashire chatted with miners' wives from South Wales ; Mansfield women warned Durham representatives what non-political unionism meant in practice ; Bradford textile workers talked to engineers' wives from the Midlands.

Every single one of the three hundred provincial delegates had made great personal sacrifice to scrape together the money for the railway fare. New clothes had been foregone, household goods sold, the rent missed, washing taken in—anything in order to seize this opportunity which only the Communist Party was prepared to give them of registering their burning resentment against capitalist oppression and Labour treachery alike.

The sight of the great procession of women and children pouring into Trafalgar Square was one which will long remain in the memories of all who saw it.

The plinth was guarded by the L.L.X., and at first it seemed impossible to crowd upon it all the banners, streamers and posters that had come from all over the country. Prominently displayed were those from the textile areas, carried by millgirls in their clogs and shawls, and from the coalfields, borne by women whose pinched, haggard faces left the great crowd under no suspicion that they were not genuine miners' wives.

The meeting was opened by Kath Duncan, who, in the name of the Communist Party, welcomed all present, and particularly the 300 women who, at great personal sacrifice, had come from the provinces to join with the Communist Party in this great mass demonstration of protest against the inhuman conditions under 12 which working women and their children are compelled to live under capitalism.

Speeches were made from two sides of the plinth by Mrs. Hargreaves (Burnley textile worker), Mrs. Maddox (Co-operative Guild), Mrs. Toombs (Bradford co-operator), Mrs. Lowther (Durham miner's wife), Mrs. Armer (Notts miner's wife), Elsie Wright (Y.C.L.), and Mrs. Campbell (L.L.X.). A tremendous welcome was given to comrade Hanna Ludewig, who brought fraternal greetings and good wishes to the women of Britain from the women of Germany.

Then came A. J. Cook, welcomed with cheer upon cheer. Appropriately enough, just as he was about to speak a magnificent contingent from Notts arrived—eighty-seven strong.

These women were warmly greeted by comrade Cook, who knows the vital part they the playing in the grim struggle against Spencerism in the Notts coalfield.

Following comrade Cook came Mrs. Nally, whose husband was dismissed from the pit on the same day that he won a seat for militant socialism on a Notts County Council from his employer. Mrs. Nally announced, amid applause, that she was ashamed to stay any longer outside the ranks of the Communist Party, and intended to celebrate International Women's Day in the best possible manner—by joining up !

She was followed by speeches from Marjorie Pollitt, J. R. Campbell and Beth Turner.

The demonstration closed with three loud and enthusiastic cheers for the Communist Party and the singing of the "Internationale."

BETHNAL GREEN SOCIAL

After the Trafalgar Square demonstration, the provincial delegates were entertained by the London Committee at Bethnal Green Town Hall. Here they were joined by many London comrades, who packed the hall to overflowing. If anything, this little, informal social was more effective and of greater value than the Trafalgar Square demonstration. Revolutionary songs and choruses were lustily sung under the leadership of comrade Rutland Boughton, while Ruby Boughton made a tremendous impression on the women by her beautiful rendering of Russian lullabies and love songs. As the delegation left one by one to catch their trains, members who, in many cases, had never made a speech before in their lives, got up to express their gratitude to the Communist Party for having made possible their expression of the hatred and bitterness which working women everywhere feel against their class enemies, whether openly in the ranks of capitalism or masquerading in Labour's army. Many women were quite overcome with emotion after the stirring events of the day. A splendid response was given to comrade Lecky's eloquent appeal to all who had supported the Communist Party on this issue to join its ranks and help and take part in its fight on every issue.

WHAT WAS RESPONSIBLE FOR THE OUTSTANDING SUCCESS OF THE DEMONSTRATION?

Fundamentally the clear, straightforward and open appeal on the part of the Communist Party to women workers of all organisations—Co-operative Guilds, Labour Women's Sections, trade union branches, etc., to line up with it on this issue. No organisation or individual who received the invitation could have been unaware that it was a Communist demonstration, and we are convinced that every woman who took part in it, did so consciously recognising that only in the policy and leadership of the Communist Party is there any inspiration or guidance for the workers in their rapidly intensifying struggles.

The first step was the calling of "united front" rank and file conferences, invitations to which were sent to all working-class organisations with women members. These conferences were held in London, Manchester, Bradford, Iiverpool, Mansfield, Nottingham and Sheffield, and in nearly every case were tremendously successful, particularly in London, where 152 delegates were present, representing Communist Party locals, Y.C.L. branches, Labour Parties, Trades Councils, Women's Sections, trade union branches, branches, Left-wing Groups, I.C.W.P.A. groups, N.U.V.C.M. branches, and no less than 33 Women's Co-operative Guilds.

At these conferences, the reasons were outlined for the holding of the demonstration on a national scale, and it was agreed that the propaganda leading up to and culminating in the campaign should centre around :

(1) The poverty of in the minefields.

(2) The attack on the textile workers.

(3) Unemployment, and the Government's new Act (assisted into being by the Parliamentary Labour Party) as affecting women.

(4) Housing and food prices (with special reference to the London flood victims).

(5) Industrial Peace.

(6) The scandals of the Pensions Act and the Audit Bill.

(7) The growing menace of war.

From these conferences, United Front Committees, representative of all sections of the movement, were set up, which met regularly during the intervening weeks and organised the preparatory detailed work of the demonstration. Undoubtedly it is largely due to the capable and energetic manner in which these committees immediately got to work, under the leadership and initiative of our Party women, that the difficulty of getting things done in so short a space of time was surmounted.

The work fell roughly into three categories : (i) publicity; (ii) finance, and (iii) organisation.

The first essential was to bring to the notice of the widest possible circle of women the information that the demonstration was to take place, and that it was open to all working women, regardless of their political beliefs, who were discontented with their pre-sent miserable conditions, were desirous of protesting against them, and prepared to fight for something better.

Circulars announcing the details of the demonstration and appealing for support were sent out to all working-class organisations, together with an offer to, send a speaker from the committee who would explain fully the aims and objects of the demonstration. The response to this last invitation was remarkable. We were besieged with so many requests for speakers that it was impossible to get all organisations satisfied.

Leaflets were got out, and distributed at factory gates, at all public meetings, put through letter-boxes, delivered by hand, put in all Party and Left-wing literature sold, and distributed by comrades canvassing during the elections.

Systematic canvassing was done with the " Working Woman," which devoted considerable space to the popularising of International Women's Day.

A big feature of the preparatory work was the number of factory-gate meetings held. This applies particularly, of course, to the textile areas, where the impending attack on hours and wages was made one of the central themes of the campaign. The Lancashire and Cheshire mill girls took a tremendous interest in the demonstration right from the start, and from two mills, delegates were actually elected to represent the workers at Trafalgar Square.

The greater part of our publicity (apart, of course, from our own press, the "Worker" and the "Sunday

Worker") was done through the medium of poster-parades and pavement-chalking, our advertisements being refused by the " Daily Herald" (which, is however, quite willing to print for mineowners and Liberal clubs).

The making of posters and the selection of slogans was undertaken very thoroughly. Suggested slogans were circularised, embracing every phase of the working woman's life. Industrial demands, home demands, local, national and international slogans were all embodied, which, in the very large number of well-organised poster-parades which were held, must have had great propaganda value, in addition to advertising the demonstration very thoroughly.

Wherever a Party, Left-wing, Minority Movement or Friends of Soviet Russia meeting or conference was held, one of our women got in for a five or ten minutes' speech on the International Women's Day demonstration. Sympathisers' meetings were held by locals or groups, street and cottage meetings were held, particularly in the mining areas, and every Party aggregate meeting was asked to devote as much time as possible to a discussion of local plans.

Closely linked up with the question of publicity was the question of finance, which was very badly needed. It had been decided to invite as our guests all women ex-class-war prisoners and the wives of the imprisoned Cramlington miners, and it was also our intention to have as the majority of our speakers, women actually living and working in the mining, textile and other important industrial areas. Then we had to remember that the women who struggled and sacrificed to come to the demonstration would have to be given hospitality while they were in London.

Subscription sheets were issued to all working-class organisations (here again the best response came from the Co-operative Guilds), to our Party locals and Y.C.L. branches. Raffles, whist-drives, jumble sales, socials, cottage teas, concerts, etc., were energetically organised to bring in money. Individuals were approached for donations, and a fund opened in the " Sunday Worker."

Sewing parties met, which first purchased the material, then made kerchiefs, bannerets, etc., which in turn were purchased by each individual.

The actual organisation of the demonstration required much care and consideration. As its popularity became increasingly evident a decision was taken to organise six contingents from the most important suburban points, to march from there to the Embankment, and thence all together to Trafalgar Square.

The Labour League of Ex-Servicemen was approached to marshal the procession, steward the demonstration and guard the plinth. The first Women's Unit of the L.L.X. also appeared in uniform for the first time, led the demonstration and stood on the plinth throughout the proceedings. The appearance of the L.L.X. caused a considerable sensation, and the greater part of the press publicity which the demonstration received was devoted to "Britain's Red Army," as the L.L.X. was usually described.

Enquiries were made at the railway stations for cheap fares for parties of women, and in all cases where a dozen or more travelled together reduced fares were obtained. Most women were compelled to travel over-night in order to arrive in time, and also return by night in order not to miss their work the next morning.

The 300 women who came from the provinces were made up of 87 from Nottinghamshire, 71 from York-shire, 50 from Lancashire and Cheshire, 25 from Birmingham, 20 from Liverpool, 20 from Brighton, 10 from South Wales, 5 from Durham, and individuals or little groups of two or three coming from districts from which it was impossible to send a representative delegation.

There is no doubt that this number could easily have been trebled if the women had had longer time to save up their fares.

CONCLUSION

The demonstration of which the story has just been told was noteworthy in that it marked a definite advance on the part of British working women towards complete class-consciousness.

The message of the Communist Party has been carried to thousands of women in every part of the country, in many cases for the first time. They have seen the Communist Party as the one militant working class party in this country, and, by working with our members during the organisational period, have had their minds cleared of many misconceptions fostered by our enemies.

That this is true is proved by the dozens of letters we have received from non-party women all over the country, expressing their gratitude to the Communist Party, stating that their sacrifices were well worth while, and that they will never forget the wonderful and inspiring sight of that great army of determined women demonstrators.

Barriers have been broken down and prejudices overcome. Thousands of women have definitely ranged themselves on the side of the Communist Party and against the Industrial Peace policy.

Pacifism is losing its grip on Britain's working women, and they will no longer be so easily cheated by illusions.

The slogans borne in the procession indicated a complete change of attitude. Reactionary Labour leaders were openly condemned, and the demand was made for action and not speeches to overthrow capitalism.

The increasing bitterness of the class struggle is forcing women out into the fight, and the only party prepared to give them a lead is the Communist Party. The only logical conclusion is for women who realise the futility and the hopelessness of reformism and pacifism to get into the ranks of the Communist Party at once, and share with us the privilege of leading our class to emancipation.

One of the most cherished illusions in this country is that we shall never have a revolution in Britain— that the temper of our workers is too easy and equable, and the Britisher too stolid and reliable ever to engage in revolution.

Apart from the historical incorrectness of this view, which refuses to take into account the revolutions that have laid the foundations of successive periods of British history, this attitude also refuses to consider the driving force of economic conditions.

It is not by propaganda alone that revolutions are made. Social revolutions have their economic foundations. These foundations are already laid.

Declining British capitalism, mortally wounded in the last great war, is trying to save itself by the increasing oppression and repression of the workers. This repression is pushed to such an extent that thousands already realise that under the old order they have nothing to hope for, but everything to gain from the new.

When a country reaches this stage it is approaching nearer to revolution. History has taught us that women are the last to become conscious of the need for revolutionary political changes, but swift to act once the need is manifest.

The beginning of all revolutions can be traced to the days when women in large masses poured on to the streets voicing their protest against the old order.

Capitalism itself has sown the seeds of revolution in this country. On March IIth, 1928, we perceived the shoots. The harvest will be gathered when millions of women, together with the men, under the leadership of the Communist Party, have fought and vanquished capitalism.

Women on the plinth, 1928

Women unemployed marchers in the 1930s

In 1930, 1932, 1934 and 1936 the National Unemployed Workers' Movement organised national marches to London by the unemployed which included contingents of women. This account of the 1936 march was written by Emmie Lawther, Deputy Leader of the march, and is in a pamphlet *Emmie Lawther: a tribute,* a copy of which can be found at the Working Class Movement Library.

Emmie started her working life in the Potteries at the age of 13. She became an active trade unionist and was a branch secretary by the time she was 18. She also joined the Social Democratic Federation.

In 1920 she went to Ruskin College for two years and then spent a year in Vienna teaching English. In 1923 she got married to Steve Lawther, whom she had met at Ruskin, and went to live in Chopwell in the North East where he was a miner. She quickly became active in the Labour Party's Women's Advisory Council.

Her husband was imprisoned for 3 months during the General Strike. Emmie was very active in the miner's relief fund distributing thousands of pounds to women for their families She also campaigned for a birth control clinic, despite the disapproval of male Labour politicians.

In 1928 she visited the Soviet Union on a delegation, going to Leningrad, Moscow and the Donbass coalfield and spoke at many meetings about what she had seen in terms of child welfare,

which exceeded what was available in Britain. She also spoke at the Women's March discussed previously.

In 1929 she attended the first International Anti-Fascist Congress in Berlin. After the Nazis came to power she took in a child refugee from Germany who later served in the British army.

In the early 1930s she was very active in the NUWM, speaking at many meetings. This is her account of the 1936 march.

Thirty-two women assembled in Coventry on the evening of Tuesday, 27th October, 1936, to take part in the National Unemployed Workers' movement.

They came from the distressed areas of Scotland, Cumberland, Tyneside, Wearside, Merseyside and the Midlands. These women knew they were on a serious mission and, though most of them had never left their homes and families before, they came because they felt it was their duty to make this protest to the Government and to bring the poverty and malnutrition rampant in the distressed areas to the notice of the people in towns, villages and hamlets on the route to London.

Not knowing what they had to face but prepared to meet any hardship such a trek may entail, the women began their march on Wednesday, 28th October, determined to persevere and reach their objective.

We set off from Lockhurst and arrived at Coventry about 10.30am. After a meeting at the Labour Exchange, we set off for Rugby, a distance of 15 miles. In an hour or so the town gave way to countryside and we passed through many pretty scenes and eventually have our mid-day meal by the roadside, sandwiches provided by the Labour and Co-operative women of Coventry. During the break we decided to have a ten minutes rest each hour as the majority of us were already feeling the effects of being "broke in" to this new life. At one of these breaks, a farmer came and gave us a sack of apples, large jug of milk and a half-crown to our collection.

We were to meet with many such kindly incidents on our journey. Long before we reached Rugby we were too tired to appreciate the glamour of the countryside, but in spite of this, we marched into this town as the workers were leaving the factories just after 5pm with banners flying and singing our marching songs and the people responded in no uncertain manner. Here,a good meal was provided by the co-operative and served in their hall where we were to sleep. We were all very tired, many had blisters on their feet, others ached in every limb but everybody endeavoured to make light of their weariness. After a sing-song and much good humoured chaff, we settled down to our second night on bare boards.

Next morning after breakfast and carrying our mid-day meal we start for Daventry in a heavy drizzle, everybody accepting the wretched weather with good philosophy. After our mid-day meal, we send our advance guard ahead, on her bike, to make arrangements for our stay in Daventry. She ultimately returns and informs me that we are to stay in the Workhouse and the Master is making soup for our arrival. Oh! How we could smell that soup during the last weary miles to Daventry.

Arriving at the Workhouse, everyone slips off her pack and makes a bee-line for the mess room. We sit down expectant, the soup is served, and eagerness gives way to dismay. Never have I seen such a concoction – a thick, lumpy, mess with bits of fat here and there. We try to eat the disgusting mess but our indefatigable leader, Maud Brown, is the only one that sticks it. She certainly set us an example, but we preferred to make a meal of the farmer's apples.

We tramped though town and village, Coventry, Rugby, Daventry, Northampton, Ampthill, St Albans, Finchley and Islington to London. Many times seeking a night's shelter in Workhouses, oft we were weary and footsore but we never faltered. We carried our message of poverty and distress from the special areas, caused by the callous indifference of the Government, to the needs of decent people, wherever we went. The

The women marchers resting

The women marchers meeting the Mayor of Islington with Emmie on the right

people were amazed at the stories of hardship, poverty and malnutrition our women had to tell. And we aroused the sympathy of all sections of the community. Many people helped to make our journey to London as light as possible.

In Coventry, Newport Pagnell, Finchley and Islington, the church loaned us their halls to sleep in and we were thankful for their kindness. We shall not forget "mine host" of the "Sow and Pigs" midway between Ampthill and Dunstable, who provided a room with a roaring fire for 32 women soaked to the skin. We arrived wet and dismal and left warm and dry with the kindliest feelings for the cheery host who had done so much for us.

We marched to London to arouse the public consciousness to the Government's attitude on unemployment. We arrived there on Saturday, 7th November, and carried out eight strenuous days of campaigning in the Metropolis.

We addressed Co-operative Guilds, Trade Union Branches, Public meetings, lobbied the House of Commons and carried out all kinds of activities. Those who saw shall never forget the Armistice Celebrations of 1936. Following the official ceremony, 2,000 marchers, who were already lined up in the Horse Guards Parade, marched into Whitehall and paraded past the Cenotaph. They were preceded by five men and five women marchers, each Group bearing a wreath from the men and women marchers that was placed at

the foot of the Cenotaph. The eerie stillness of the morning was broken by a cheer as those two wreaths were placed in position and the huge procession that had marched from every part of the isles now marched past the Cenotaph and re-forming ranks. It was a most impressive sight.

Our march was essentially a protest against the National Government. When the first contingents had taken the road five weeks previously, the Cabinet issued a statement, deprecating the march and informing us that they would not meet the marchers. After our arrival in London, Mr Baldwin repeated this declaration in the House of Commons but we broke through this conspiracy and forced the Minister of Labour to meet a deputation from the Marchers before we had concluded a week's campaign in London. Not only did we break throughthe ban of the National Government but we broke through all the bans of officialdom in our movement and we achieved a measure of unity undreamed of at Edinburgh a few months before. I myself spoke on the same platform at Sir Stafford Cripps, G R Strauss, MP, Wal Hannington and Arthur Horner.

The demonstration in Hyde Park on Sunday, 8th November, was one of the greatest ever seen on that historic ground; it brought on to the same platform Clem Attlee, Leader of the Parliamentary party, Wal Hannington, Leader of the Unemployed, and a host of Members of

Parliament and Trade Union Leaders and left wing leaders who would not have associated on the same platform a short time ago. We can claim the march achieved a measure of unity never before accomplished and that basis that we laid will bear fruit in the future.

Emmie remained active for next thirty years. She died in 1965.

Our thanks to the Working Class Movement Library for the pictures.

Nurses' March, 15th August 1968

This march was organised by Sister Patricia Veal who worked as an administrative sister at South Western Hospital in Stockwell, London. In July 1968 she had read about nurses lobbying MPs over pay, went along to the House of Commons but found no other nurses there. She decided to organise a march and spent £6 on sending letters to every hospital in the country. According to Patricia, some letters were intercepted by matrons. "I had one letter from a matron saying that she wouldn't let her nurses read such stuff. We're going to frame it." She also said that the whole edifice of nursing was tottering. "Florence Nightingale would have 50 fits if she saw how nursing is now." Patricia was critical of the Royal College of Nursing which she said was "all talk and no action" and "not for the ordinary nurse."

Her efforts paid off. On 15th August 1968 Patricia led a march of 1,000 or so nurses from Marble Arch to 10 Downing Street where they delivered a letter to the Prime Minister Harold Wilson. They included nurses from nine London teaching hospitals, as well hospitals in Sussex, Surrey and Derbyshire.

Some hospitals had tried to stop nurses attending by refusing them time off. In some cases nurses had been forbidden to wear their uniforms, but many marched in the uniforms they used for private cases. Some marched barefoot: one nurse from India marched in her sari.

The nurses marched six-a-breast down Park Laneunder the slogan "Unite and Fight" and carried banners that read "There's a curse on the purse of every nurse" and "Wait till you get a hernia – Mr Wilson". They sang songs about bedpans and bad food to the time of "John Brown's Body" and "We all live on bread and margarine" to the tune of the Beatles' song "Yellow Submarine." In Whitehall the march paused while Patricia fixed her hair. Finally, on arrival at Downing Street, a petition was delivered by Patricia, along with two colleagues from the same hospital, Sister Tina Stone and Sister Mary Chundee:

We are dissatisfied not only because of the latest salary increase which was consumed by the latest increases in board and lodging, National Health contributions, income tax, and superannuation but we are equally concerned over working conditions resulting in the loss of so many nurses. We believe that the National Health Service is wasting money and that many departments need reorganising and streamlining.

After the march Patricia announced, "Now, there's going to be no turning back. We're going to form an association to keep this up!" She and a number of other nurses held a meeting in one of their flats on 22nd August and set upthe United Nurses' Association.

Seven of the organisers were interviewed by Penny Adams for an article which appeared in the *Aberdeen Evening Express*, under the heading "Why those nurses marched to Downing Street." (*The Magnificent Seven* was a Western - based on the 1954 Japanese film *The Seven Samurai* - released in 1960, which started Yul Brynner.)

Triumphant tears filled the "Magnificent Seven's eyes as they led 1500 cheering nurses to Downing Street to demand a better deal for nurses. Later, "The Seven"—hospital sisters from South Western Hospital, Brixton —put their feet up, sipped coffee, and told me about the nurses' lot...This what they want:

Patient care.

Better Conditions for Nurses, Trained and Untrained.

More realistic salaries from nurses to matrons.

Why do these married women feel they have to form the "Nurses Unite and Fight Committee" and lead the first nurses' march in history to fight for their colleagues in uniform?

"The Royal College of Nurses (the nurses body) are old women," said attractive 33-year-old Sister Tina Stone. "They are not practising nurses. They have their heads in the ground."

Red-haired Sister Patricia Veal (33) thought up the idea of their march. When she went to lobby her MP about nurses' conditions of work, she found she was the only one there. Her reaction was: "I am going organise a protest" and the six others joined her.

Springing from their three protest points are pleas for more time to give to the patients, more realistic shift hours and better pay. Much of this boils down to a bigger allocation of nurses each hospital.

Here is a typical day in a hospital ward nurses life (which every nurse goes through some time in her career):

7.30 am Start. Give patients their breakfast.
8 am Bedpan round.
8.15 am Bedmaking.
9 am Medicines.
9.30am to 10.30am Nurses' coffee break aken In rota.
10am Dressings, injections, etc., patients' coffee time.
12 noon. Doctors' round.

(In between this comes answering relatives' call, dealing with relatives of danger-list patients, looking after ill patients, bed-making, commoding, walking patients to toilet, doing dentures, mouths, sponging down patients with high temperatures, taking temperatures and blood pressures, possibly blood transfusions and drops of all kinds.)

12 noon. Patients' lunch (including feeding ill patients and feeding children in toddlers' ward)
12.30 pm to 2pm Nurses' take lunch on rota.
12.45pm Bedpan round, washing bowls, doing backs, making beds.
1pm Medicines.
2pm Visiting times – nurses tidy trays, cupboards, etc.
3pm. Patients' teatime. Bedpans, backs, bedpans, etc.
5pm Evening treatments, backs, bedpans, etc.
6pm – 6.30pm Patients' suppers.
7pm Visiting time – nurses tidy up, clean bathrooms, sluices, etc. Nurse in charge writes out report for night staff and fills in details for each patients' day report.
8pm Night staff arrive.

This is just one shift, but others are: 7-30am-5pm (for student nurses). 7.30am-1.30pm and back again for 5pm-8pm, 10am-8pm 7.30am-6pm, 7.30am-10am and back again for 8pm. "The shift system never got off the ground because we never had enough staff,' said Sister Stone. "By the time nurses have got home – if they live outside the hospital they are either too tired or it is too late to out anywhere. "

Also, most nurses' hostels have curfew time for nurses ranging from 11pm to 1pm. Very often, say the sisters, a nurse has insufficient time to talk and sympathise with patients and advise student nurses hospital problems.

On pay, student nurses get £7 per week (living out) and £4 clear (living in). They should get £10 a week in their pockets after deductions, say "The Seven Staff nurses should have a starting rate of £1,000 a year, sisters should get about £2000 a year after a qualifying period of three months, according to experience.

The sisters feel a nurser, to which married nurses could bring their children at hospitals, would encourage a return of nurses

Now the "Magnificent Seven" are trying get details of other aspects of nursing, district, midwifery, etc.— for guidance In their bid improve conditions all fields of the profession. "We want everyone to write to us, giving their troubles, their woes and their possible remedies," said committee secretary, Sister Jean Baxter.

And the future?

"I am very happy with the march," said Its leader, Sister Veal. "This is only the beginning of things and you will see a great change. You can't sack everyone. They need us. If they decide to dismiss, sack or victimise us. the patients will suffer because there will be really acute shortage nurses if they start doing this." This is the nurses' lot and this is what they are fighting for...

The UNA continued its agitation. On 13th December 1968 Patricia and 14 other nurses went to the House of Commons. It seems very likely that this action was deliberately timed to coincide with the 50th anniversary of the General Election held on 14th December 1918 in which some women voted for the first time.

They arrived at 9.45am and, to begin with, confined themselves to giving out leaflets which described small hospitals as being full of "antiques" like furniture, matrons, ward sisters; senior administrators who lacked the courage to face reality; and unions who were trying to lower nursing standards; and unsatisfactory working conditions. Patricia told the press it was too cold to chain themselves to the railing so they were going to go in and tell MPs "a few home truths instead."

The women went inside to sit in the public gallery from where they heard Jo Grimond deliver a speech

Nurses on the March, 15th August 1968 (Topfoto)

about Shetland ponies. After he had finished Patricia jumped up and addressed the Chamber for 30 seconds on their demands, in the spirit of Muriel Matters, who in October 1908 also made a speech to the Chamber after chaining herself to a grille in the Ladies' Gallery. Patricia shouted. "I want to talk on behalf of the nurses. The nurses want support. Listen to the nurses. The nurses want to fight for the patients of this country. Will MPs listen instead of talking about ponies?"

The nurses somewhat half-heartedly tried to emulate the suffragettes by tying themselves together with bits of string. The Serjeant-at-Arms, Rear Admiral A H C Gordon-Lennox, took them into custody and they were detained "at the Speaker's pleasure" in a small, cold room. They were eventually let out at 1.30 pm on condition they did not cause a disturbance within a mile of Westminster. Patricia told the press that the MPs had been talking "a load of drivel about Shetland ponies" so when she had spoken "all the MPs woke up".

The UNA staged a protest on 22nd April 1969 outside the Department of Health and Social Security with 150 nurses singing "Why Are We Waiting." Patrica told the press, "We want this system abolished. These girls are hungry." After five minutes the Secretary of State himself, Richard Crossman, came out to speak to them. He said that nurses had their own representatives who were negotiating on their behalf. He suggested

that rather than stand in the cold wind, they send in a delegation. This was done, with a small delegation going in to speak to Lady Serota, a Minister, for an hour. Patricia told the Minister that some student nurses were struggling to eat.

On 15th May 1969 the UNA staged a protest outside the Royal College of Nursing whom they accused of "sweeping so much dirt under the carpets" with Patricia wielding a broom before the cameras of the press.

After 1970 the UNA faded away with Patricia Veal last heard in 1976 of running a private nursing agency in Tooting Bec.

Equal Pay March, 18th May 1969
The 1960s and early 1970s witnessed an unprecedented explosion of industrial militancy. Most of the strikes were in male–dominated industries, but there was one strike by women which was significant and attracted national attention. This was by 187 women who worked sewing the seat covers at the Fords car plant in Dagenham, Essex. It began on 7th June 1968 and lasted until 28th June.

The women walked out when they were informed that as part of the regrading process their jobs were regarded as grade B (less skilled) instead of the more skilled category C (which of course was applied to the jobs done by men. In addition they were paid 15% less than the men on the B grade. The women were joined in the strike by the machinists at Halewood near Liverpool, often overlooked.

Without the finished seats Fords quickly ground to a halt. On 28th June the strikers' delegation met the Secretary of State for Employment, Barbara Castle, and negotiated an end to the dispute. The women did not get equal pay with the men: instead they would receive 92% instead of 85%.

The strike at Fords had an effect on the emerging women's movement and women in the trade union movement. In an article on "The Beginnings of Women's Liberation in Britain," historian and feminist Sheila Rowbotham later wrote:
The Fords strike sent a tremor of hope through the trade union movement. Women who had fought hopelessly at TUC meetings for equal pay took heart again. There followed a period of industrial militancy among women workers which has only sporadically been chronicled in the socialist press, and has never been seriously studies. Rose Boland was undoubtedly right when she said "I think the Ford women have definitely shaken the women of the country."

Janet Blackman commented in an article in the 1969 edition of *Trade Union Register* that:
The strike of nearly 400 Ford women machinists at Dagenham and Halewood last summer lifted the old boring subject of the unequal treatment of women on to a different plane. Yes, boring, because of the rut into which the campaign had stuck...The Ford women machinists swung the debate about women's rights away from the concerns - albeit very real problems - of the middle class and professional women to those of the woman worker, successfully perhaps for the first time since the match girls' strike of 1888. By September, 1968 the TUC was passing a resolution supporting industrial action as a possible means of obtaining equal pay. Janet

In the wake of the strike an organisation called the National Joint Action Committee for Women's Equal Rights (NJACC) was set up with a number of groups around the country and organised a march, calling for equal pay which took place in London on 18th May 1969, assembling at Temple tube station and marching to Hyde Park. About 1,000 attended. Sheila Rowbotham reported on it for the Marxist newspaper *Black Dwarf*:

The sight of this far from typical demonstration aroused considerable interest amongst on-lookers not only because it was headed by a pipe-band but because of the predominance of women. In Trafalgar Square drenched figures stood resolutely under a canopy of umbrellas listening to the speakers, who included Agnes McLean, AEF shop steward from Glasgow, Rose Boland from Fords, Christine Page, Audrey Wise from USDAW, Ernie Roberts and Fred Blake from AEF and NUVB were there to extend solidarity to the women in the struggle for equal pay. AEF, USDAW, SOGAT, NUUB banners were on the plinth. The speakers stressed how half the women employed are getting less than 5s an hour, how there are 4 million women getting less than £10 a week.

Agnes McLean made the important point for socialists on equal pay when she stated that it should not be defined as equal pay at the expense of male workers. She said "We're not asking for a share in the exploitation of the men. We are asking for it from the shareholders."

Some of the slogans women had improvised on the NJACC official placards it more bluntly.

BARBARA GETS HERS WHY NOT US?

And

**GONE IS THE VICTORIAN AGE
WHEN WOMEN USED TO PLAY
NOW WE'RE WORKING BLOODY HARD
SO GIVE US EQUAL PAT**

A woman from the Post Office Engineers in Enfield held up

WE WANT A CHANCE TO PROVE WE CAN DO THE WORK OF ANY MAN

"All my own work," she commented as I scribbled it down. Pottery workers from Stoke on Trent carried

**EQUAL PAY NOW
WE MAKE MUGS BUT WE ARE NOT MUGS**

They told us it was the first demonstration they'd ever been on. They thought more women would have come but they were a bit nervous demonstrating. "You hear such funny things about what goes on at them." They'd been to conferences before. If it was possible to get enough women involved, and the men saw they had a movement, they felt sure they'd stand by them. Part of the problem was women often found it difficult to speak up at union meetings. They'd formed women advisory groups in their lodge which met as well as general lodge meetings within the National Union of Pottery Workers. This helped women to work out their

The Ford women strikers, June 1968

problems at work and put a case to the men in the union. Transport workers stressed the importance of the men's support and referred to the hostility of some of their men over the issue of women drivers.

Rose Greenford said they were now putting the demand of equal sick pay. For a man this is granted after he's worked for a year. Women have to wait five years. They thought they'd be able to get this through.

The odd hostile man popped up. One bespectacled man suddenly became the centre of an angry group of very small women, who prodded him indignantly and were supported by a great mountain of a man with a red face and black beret. The bespectacled man became most embarrassed and obviously regretted having created the confrontation. "WE WORK FOR YOU. YOU LIVE OFF US" shouted the girls. "Sock it to him" said a young policeman watching with delight.

A policewoman, asked whether she had equal pay, refused to comment. But two policemen said policewomen worked less hours. They did a different kind of work which couldn't compared. Policemen should get danger money. *Dwarfs* offered solidarity for a police demo.

Everyone I talked to felt this was only the beginning. The movement for EQUAL PAY NOW is going to get bigger, noisier and more

determined. And it's not just about equal pay. You can't challenge the economic subordination of women without immediately highlighting the total secondary social position.

Something is stirring.

Something which has been silent for a long time.

As it turned out this was the only marchd organised by NJACC. As series of rallies were planned for 12th September 1969 as part of a National Equal Pay Day but these was cancelled and just a a single rally was held in Conway Hall, London, at which Sister Patricia Veal from the United Nurses Association was the main speaker. After that NJACC does not seem to have held any further events.

Women's Liberation march, 6th March 1971
Women Liberation in Britain emerged in 1969 with a handful of groups meeting in London. In February 1970 the first national conference took place in Oxford. The organisers expected a 100 women to attend ; in fact, over 600 turned up. The movement now spread across the country.

Another key milestone was the first Women's Liberation march which took place on 6th March 1971 in London (in freezing weather, it should be noted). Organised by the Women's National Co-ordinating Committee and Ad Hoc Committee for the London March 6th Demonstration it assembled at Speakers' Corner and marched to Trafalgar Square.

The idea was to bring women together in support of

the four demands of the Women's Liberation movement:

Free abortion and contraception on demand
Equal educational and job opportunities
Free 24-hour nurseries
Equal pay

The event was planned with a good deal of imagination with banners proclaiming "Women Unite" and "Women's Liberation", a twelve foot Old Woman's Shoe, a caged woman (Mis-Stress) as well as co-ordinated singing, dancing and music and performances at the end in Trafalgar Square.

Surviving footage captures its fun aspect and the sometimes bewildered reactions of passers-by. Around 3,000 women and men attended.

An article in the Women's Liberation Workshop newsletter *Shrew* reflected on what had been achieved – and, perhaps more importantly, not achieved:
Male passer-by: What do you want – Stuffing?

Woman in uniform: "We're not allowed to think..."

Woman in fur coat: "abortion makes me turn cold. It's like shutting the stable door after the horse has bolted. "

Middle-aged woman shop assistant: "I think I'm in favour."

These remarks of bystanders at the demonstration on Saturday, and the attitude of amused tolerance in the press coverage of the march, must guide us in assessing exactly what we have achieved. The demonstration raises certain questions about our aims and strategy as a movement. That over 3,000 women assembled in Hyde Park prepared to march despite falling snow and freezing temperatures was reason enough for spirits to be high. Not only the numbers present, but that these represented nation-wide support for our cause must be an encouragement. While we need to stand united in the face of press criticism of the demonstration and of the movement as a whole, it is important that our first experience of a national demonstration should provoke self-criticism within the movement.

What were we "demonstrating": was this a demonstration of women's solidarity or was it an outing? Was it a march, or a wander through the West End? In terms of appearances a useful comparison is the New York Women's Liberation demonstration of September 1970. Several thousand women, arms linked and chanting slogans, surged down Park Avenue, sweeping aside police attempting to restrict the marchers to two traffic lanes. Police had barricaded sidewalks to keep public and demonstrators apart, and crowds gathered to watch the spectacle – expecting a circus. But, infected by the determination of the marchers, middle-aged women left their husbands and girls ducked under the barricades to join the march when challenged to do so. The uncommitted were made to feel that something important concerning them was at stake.

Given the British spirit of moderation in all things, in contrast with the polarisation on equivalent issues in American society, and that the British woman clings more conventionally to the passivity of her traditional role – did we, in marching, really provoke or inspire women "on the side" to commit themselves? Many, questioned on their attitude to the march, came out in favour of at least two or three of the four demands in point but had not been made to feel to demonstrate solidarity on the issues. Much more is at stake in the Women's Liberation movement than equal pay, equal educational opportunities, state nurseries, free abortion and contraception: the underlying factor is the liberation of woman for independent self-determination as a human being. To quote a hand-out distributed on the march, "Social reforms do not necessarily mean a change in attitudes." Female emancipation cannot be achieved simply by legislation as female suffrage has shown.

If all we were doing on March 6th was demanding social welfare changes with which many can agree without any fundamental changes in their conception of and attitude to "woman", what was the real confrontation of this demonstration?

We must avoid putting ourselves in a position in which we can be fobbed off with superficial concessions and be left with nothing more to say.

All women must be confronted with the fact that the liberation of women requires a fundamental revision of the definitions of all human roles in society. This raises the question of the role of male support of the movement: on one hand, their presence on Saturday gives weight to the liberated men and women through the call to

Women's Liberation march, 6th March 1971

women to do something about their own position. On the other hand, the presence of husbands and boyfriends in the midst of "women united" made us more vulnerable to jokey press comments and public amusement – and possible identification by the public as yet another group of "student revolutionaries," rather than as an unprecedented assembly of women, demonstrating in the cause of all women.

If we failed to communicate the seriousness of the aims of Women's Liberation perhaps we should ask ourselves whether our future efforts to communicate should now involve a choice. One alternative is uncompromising militancy which must of neccessity provoke commitment or hostility to the movement, but which brings to light fundamental and radical issues implied by women's liberation. Or do we try to appeal to the mass of women in this country at the moment who think they are in favour – thus achieving a real following but running the risk of making the four demands an end in themselves.

The moderate method could be regarded as first step towards greater things, or as the removal of specific grievances, but at the possible cost of true liberation.

Women and Men?

Many men were on our demonstration - probably a quarter of the demonstrators. Parts of the movement either say "Of course we don't hate men, it's not men against women, it's capitalism of course, we don't hate men, t;s not men against women it's capitalism or define those of still living with men as not really revolutionary. or define those of us still living with men as not really revolutionary. We are challenging the old roles between men and women. It seems to me that we need to begin, in dialogue with any men who are interested, to try to define new patterns, to build new structures, FROM OUR OWN POLITICS, for their participation and contribution to the battle for a new society. Isn't it inconsistent to say we are for men sharing in the raising of children and not to give any lead to how this sharing can be done? Or to denounce women who are trying to work this out? All relationships in this society are compromising: we are old people trying to make a new society. How do we start, together, without denying all the options we say we are fighting for?

Dare To be Free: a play about Mary Quaile

In 2016 the Mary Quaile Club commissioned a play about Mary Quaile which was called *Dare To Be Free*. Bernadette Hyland, one of the founders of the Club, explained: "We thought that a play about Mary would be a wonderful way of making her life and work as a trade union organiser better known to a new generation. This play is not be an exercise in cosy historical nostalgia, but will directly link Mary's work in organising workers in the early C20th to the conditions faced by many workers today ie low pay, zero hours and the hostility by many employers towards the very idea of trade unions."

The production was made possible by donations from the following trade unions: BECTU, Chartered Society of Physiotherapists, Communication Workers Union, Fire Brigades Union (Region No 5), General Federation of Trade Unions, Bristol branch of NUJ, Calderdale branch of NUJ, Glasgow branch of NUJ, Manchester and Salford branch of NUJ, the Professional Footballers' Association, Bolton branch of NUT, Bolton branch of UNISON, and UNITE (North West region).

We also received donations from a number of individuals: Geoff and Judy Brown, Christopher Eccleston, John Finch, Tony Garnett, Gaynor Lloyd, Rita Machin, Maxine Peake, Sheila Rowbotham, Margret Ward.

Dare To Be Free was set in the past and present. It's 1908 and waitresses in a Manchester cafe are fed up and ready to strike for proper pay and decent working conditions. It's 2016 and workers in a Manchester "fast food experience" are fed up and ready to strike for proper pay and decent working conditions. Linking the two eras is Mary Quaile, come to help out her modern-day sisters because the issues she fought on 100 years ago are back with vengeance...

The play was written by Jane McNulty, whose previous work included writing episodes for *EastEnders*, *Doctors, Peak Practice*, and *Heartbeat*. It was directed by Bill Hopkinson, who taught at Edge Hill University. The song with which the play ends "Dare to Be Free" was written by Carol Donaldson.

Mary Quaile was played by Catherine Kinsella, while the waitresses in 1908 and 2016 were played by Rebecca Brown, Rachel Priest and Catarina Pinto Soromenho.

The play was premiered on Saturday 30th April at the Mechanics Institute, Manchester as part of the May Day Festival. There were three other performances:

Saturday 14th May 2pm, Inspire Café, Inspire Centre, Levenshulme

Sunday 15th May, 2pm Glossop Labour Club, Glossop.

Saturday 4th June 3.30pm, Three Minute Theatre Afflecks Arcade, Oldham Street, Manchester. This final performance was part of the launch of our pamphlet about Mary Quaile and modern day women in trade unions, also called *Dare To Be Free.*

Bernadette Hyland spoke first, outlining the facts of Mary's Quaile's life as a trade unionist and her role in organising women into unions, first in Manchester and then nationally. She drew parallels with 2016 in which we are fighting the same battles for basic rights at work as Mary and others did 100 years ago. Bernadette ended her speech by quoting from Jane Stewart from Unite, one of the women she interviewed for the publication: "After thirty years I want to encourage other people to get involved in the trade union movement. If we don't fight we will never succeed. Too often things get worse because people do nothing, so not fighting is not an option."

The next speaker was Sarah Woolley from the Bakers' Union. She spoke about how she had become involved in the union after experiencing problems at work. She was asked by the union to become a shop steward and is now a full-time officer. It had changed her life in so many ways. Sarah said that if she could do it "then anyone could."

We then welcomed our final speakers – Khadija, Robert and Ana from the Hotel Workers branch of Unite – who had come up from London that morning especially to speak at our event. They spoke about their own experiences at work and as members of Unite. It was often difficult to organise workers in hotels or in cafes and restaurants, but the union was making steady progress, offering advice and support, as well as educational opportunities such as English classes. However union activists were often targeted by managers determined to keep unions out of their businesses.

Pictures from the launch of *Dare To be Free* at Three Minute Theatre

Cast

Mary Quaile:	30s, a Manchester working-class woman. Plain, serviceable clothes (long black skirt, a jacket, flat shoes, a hat.)
Waitress 1:	student.
Waitress 2:	single mother
Waitress 3:	migrant worker

The play is set in the present (2016) and in 1926 & 1908.

> MEETING HALL.
>
> A TRESSLE TABLE, FOUR CHAIRS.
>
> WAITRESS 1 AND WAITRESS 3 (MODERN UNIFORMS) ARRANGE CHAIRS, WIPE DOWN TABLES ETC: THEY MAY SERVE REFRESHMENTS. THEY GO ABOUT THEIR DUTIES UNOBTRUSIVELY.
>
> WAITRESS 1 GETS A TEXT, TAKES OUT HER MOBILE.

WAITRESS 1:   *(reads)* 'Sunday. Day shift. OK?'

Shit!

I've made arrangements. I promised the fam I'd get over to see them this weekend. Go Friday after lectures, catch up with a few mates, see my mum and dad. Get fed for a change. Then back Sunday morning and finish that essay. That was the plan.

But it's nine hours plus tips. And I can't turn that down, can I?

If I did? They'd take my name off the rota. And it's not like there's that many jobs going. *(sends reply)* 'OK'.

WAITRESS 3:   The security guard got knifed last night. The police came, and an ambulance. They took him away.

It was terrible. I thought we maybe would all die.

One of the other women - she comes from... I don't always get what she says: someplace there was war, bad fighting - afterwards I couldn't find her. I figured she'd gone home. Then I saw her shoe, under the sinks. She got herself in there somehow, hiding.

I wondered later maybe she was hiding from the police.

I don't know if the man is OK.

A sandwich shop. I don't want to go back to work there.

> WAITRESS 2 ARRIVES, MANOEUVERING A BABY BUGGY.

WAITRESS 2:   I know, I know, all right? Taking a baby on the bus that time of night! But I pay my fare, same as the rest of you, so you can just do one. I know that look on your faces, judging me. 'Bad mother! That child should be at home, tucked up asleep, poor little thing.' And yes, she's crying.

She's knackered. We both are.

And you know what? I agree with you. What sort of person would put a tired child through that journey so late at night?

One that doesn't have any choice.

WAITRESS 2 STOWS THE BUGGY AND HELPS THE OTHERS.

WAITRESS 1: It's eight o'clock start and Sundays there's no bus, so it'll have to be a taxi. Meaning I'm six quid down before I start. Taxi's late. He's been to the airport and there was a hold-up on the motorway, blah, blah. Like I'm even listening: I've been up half the night working on that bloody essay.

Which isn't going well, thanks for asking. So I'm late. Only ten minutes, but the duty manager's giving me evils. What time do I call this and do I think they're running some sort of charity?

As if. She says she's docking me half an hour.

Great.

MARY QUAILE ENTERS CARRYING A STOCK OF WHITE CARD AND BLACK MARKER PENS FOR PLACARDS.

WAITRESS 2: Eight till six, a little one to see to and four buses to negotiate – it's hard enough. Then the owner goes and sacks two of the staff. Said the café wasn't taking enough, that the rest of us would have to cover the hours, and I'd have to start at seven from now on.

I say to him, 'How am I going to get here for seven?'

I've got to drop my little girl at the sitter's first.' He says. 'If you don't like the hours, there's plenty who will.'

MARY: Ah, you're here already. Good, good. Good crowd.

And you found the place all right? *(herself)* Mary.

Great to see you, sister, brother.

MARY HANDS OUT CARD AND PENS TO THE AUDIENCE. AS SHE DOES SO

MARY (CONT'D): Would you take one *(the sheets of card)* and pass the rest along? Thanks, love. And the pens, if you'd pass them round too? Thank you.

WAITRESS 3: Twelve hours Friday, twelve hours Saturday.

Finish four a.m, maybe five, then clear up

Sometimes there is horrible mess and we have to clean it. On the floor, the windows. People are drunk and then are sick; throw food around, behave like monkeys in a zoo. Disgusting. The manager says we must just get on with it, it's what happens in these places.

MARY: We're going to need placards for the march, lots of them. Do you think you could write the slogans?

WAITRESS 1: I write up the specials board, wipe down the tables. A couple come in for coffee and toast; three blokes order the full English. It's a bit quiet. Half nine she comes over and tells me I'm not needed; there's enough staff on

	and I can go. Just like that.
MARY:	No need to do it right this minute. You can do it while the meeting is going on. Something with a bit of a punch, eh, bit of thunder? Really get the word out there. There'll be plenty of inspiration, I'm sure.
WAITRESS 2:	The sitter pulls a face when I tell her. She says I've still got to make sure the baby's ad something to eat before I bring her. Like she couldn't give a child a bowl of cereal?
WAITRESS 3:	Sometimes on my shift there is only me who speaks English. I have to help the others, explain the orders. The customers get impatient, then they get angry. The manager has two, three shops to look over, so isn't there to help. Sometimes customers say horrible things to us. When I first started working here I didn't know the words, but I understood OK. Hatred has only one language.
	One of the other workers - she was from Eritrea - a customer spat at her, said she was going to beat her head. For no other reason than she didn't understand straight away what the customer wants.
MARY:	We'll maybe give it few minutes, shall we, see if there's any stragglers? I think there'll be plenty join us along the road.
WAITRESS 1:	An hour's pay and that's it. Minus the taxi fare. I'd been banking on getting something at work - and there's just over a quid left on the electric. (*counts coins*) One pound and five, ten, eleven. Enough for a cheeseburger. Or fries. Not both. And I'd stayed up half the night to finish that essay.
MARY:	Meetings? I was brought up on them. Even as a baby, I'd be taken along. My mother used to say I had my union card before I had my baptismal certificate.
	I don't remember, of course - I was only three when we left Dublin to come to Manchester - but in my mind's eye I'm there with my da, helping give out pamphlets.
WAITRESS 2:	Closing time, there's just two of us to clean up. I need to go but I can't leave the other girl to do it all, can I? By the time we've done, it's nearly seven. I'm panicking. The bus is crowded, no seats. By the time I reach the sitter's it's way past baby's bedtime and she's cranky. The sitter's cranky too. 'I'll help anybody out,' she says, 'but you're taking advantage.' She's after another hour's money. Tough.
MARY:	My father, James Quaile - did you ever hear of him?
	Bricklayer. Big union man, he was. Dead now, may he rest in peace, though with all that's going on now, another lock out and workers' rights eroded, I doubt he'll be resting much. He was a union man through and through. The Ancient Guild of Incorporated Brick and Stone Layers Trade Union, to give it its full title. Which he did. He believed in "stand up and be counted". He brought us up the same. And he taught us to stand with those who were fighting for their rights.
WAITRESS 3:	The manager promised I would be trained. I had to pay one

hundred pounds for the training book.

It was a lot of money but I have to do this training so I borrow the money from my family back home. But there was no training, just told to read the book and watch the others, I'll learn. A hundred pounds for that!

I tell my family I pass the course with merit, that I am doing well and soon I will send money. I tell them that I am top chef here in Manchester.

I don't say it is sandwich shop.

WAITRESS 2: It's eight o'clock by the time we get home. I warm us up some soup but the little one is too tired to eat and by the time we've had the usual battle – 'here comes the aeroplane', which doesn't work anyway – mine's cold. I put her to bed then do some washing, tidy up. Fifteen hours after I started work and I've not sat down yet.

And I've got it all to do again tomorrow.

> THE WAITRESSES CHANGE INTO CAPS AND APRONS, THE
> UNIFORM OF THE CEYLON CAFÉ WAITRESSES
> C.1908. WAITRESS 2 GOES OFF. OVER THIS

MARY: I was twelve when I started work. Kitchen maid in one of the big houses around Manchester, owned by bankers, mill owners, cotton merchants, factory owners. Four shillings and sixpence a week, and a room at the top of the house that I shared with two other girls. It was hard work. Up at five and sometimes midnight before we'd done, seven days a week.

There was another girl, Lizzie. Tiny, a pale little wisp of a girl: said she was thirteen but she didn't look it. She slept in the attic room too. Cried every night for her mother. I used to reach out and hold her hand till she fell asleep, like I used to do with my sister when she was small. There's something in the touch of a hand, even in the dark, that brings comfort, strength.

One day, Lizzie was carrying a full tureen of soup when she slipped. Terrible mess she was in, blisters all down her front and her legs. They dismissed her.

No sick pay, nothing. They even docked her wages to pay for the broken tureen.

One thing I found really galling was having to 'give room'. Like, you're going about your work and you encounter a member of the family. You were supposed to avert our eyes until they'd gone by.

That was bad enough, but then this new housekeeper came in. Piece of work, she was! She instructed us to turn our face to the wall to give room. Like we were ashamed or something. Well, I wasn't ashamed, and I refused to pretend otherwise. So that was me down the road.

When I got home and told my father what had happened, he said I'd done right. He said a day's work was one thing, and fair enough, but no one should be humiliated. But when I told him they'd withheld my pay due to my insolence, well Da said they weren't getting away with that.

He walked me back to the house. Right to the front door, too. No tradesman's entrance for him. The housekeeper was fetched and I told her I had come for the money I was owed. I stood my ground, and Da stood beside me till that money was in my hand.

    THE CEYLON CAFÉ, 1908: WAITRESS 1 & WAITRESS 3 ARE
    FINISHING THEIR MEAL BREAK.

MARY (CONT'D)	I got a job as a waitress in a café in the centre of Manchester. Wages weren't much better. We were living in Fallowfield at that time and my brother John had fixed me up a bicycle - he was handy like that - so, weather permitting, I'd cycle to work and save my tram fare. I enjoyed the feeling of freedom, too. WAITRESS 1: My feet are killing me.
WAITRESS 3:	New shoes?
WAITRESS 1:	Would I be daft enough to break in new shoes on the job? And who can afford new shoes anyway? No, I'd no money for the tram this morning.
WAITRESS 3:	And you've walked? All that way?
WAITRESS 1:	Aye. And I'll be walking back tonight too.
WAITRESS 3:	Why don't you ask Mr Bloom for a sub against your wages?
WAITRESS 1:	When have you ever known that miserable beggar let anyone have a sub?
WAITRESS 3:	Shhh, what if he hears you?
WAITRESS 1:	He won't, he's still in his office with Dolly.
WAITRESS 3:	Only time she's ever been late in three years and she walks straight into him. He'll cut her a bit of slack though, won't he, given her ircumstances?

    WAITRESS 2 ENTERS, TEARFUL.

WAITRESS 1:	Pigs'd fly before he'd show any bit of kindness.
	(indicates DOLLY's arrival) Hush...
	What's he said, Dolly?
WAITRESS 2:	He's docked me a day's pay.
WAITRESS 1:	For ten minutes?
WAITRESS 3:	Didn't you tell him about having to drop your little one off at your mother's?
WAITRESS 2:	He wouldn't take no excuses. And I was late, there's no getting round it.
WAITRESS 3:	Did you offer to stay on to make up the time?
WAITRESS 2:	He was having none of it. Said he was going to make an example of me.
WAITRESS 1:	That miserable so and so! Knowing your husband's an invalid, and that you're the family bread winner? It's outrageous, that's what it is.
WAITRESS 2:	How am I going to manage, girls? What am I going to tell my Wilf?
WAITRESS 1:	*(to Dolly)* Come on. *(To Waitress 3)* You an' all.
WAITRESS 3:	Where we going?

80

WAITRESS 1:	To see Bloom. I'll put a bloom on his cheeks all Oh no, no, I don't want a fuss.
WAITRESS 1:	What he's done isn't fair. He can't get away with it.
WAITRESS 3:	She's right, Dolly. It's not fair.
WAITRESS 2:	You'll lose your jobs. And I will too, and I can't afford to do that. Just let it be. It's not your fight.
WAITRESS 1:	Not today it's not, but tomorrow, next week? We've got to stick together.
MARY:	None of us could afford to lose a day's pay, and Dolly had a family to support. But what the boss had done was wrong.

MARY HANDS PLACARDS TO THE THREE WAITRESSES.

WAITRESS 1:	Your waitress needs enough to feed herself too!
WAITRESS 2:	Don't stomach unfair treatment!
WAITRESS 3:	Low pay is off the menu!
MARY:	We came out on strike. And though we got quite a bit of abuse from passers-by.
WAITRESS 1:	Get back to work, lazy articles!
WAITRESS 2:	Ought to be ashamed of yourselves.
WAITRESS 3:	Should be grateful you've got a job.
MARY:	And they threw stuff at us: rotten tomatoes, even horse droppings
WAITRESS 1:	*(ducks)* Call that a throw?
MARY:	though we did also get some support.

WAITRESS 1 PICKS UP A NEWSPAPER.

WAITRESS 1:	We're in the newspaper, girls.

THE WAITRESSES READ OVER HER SHOULDER.

WAITRESS 1 (CONT'D):	"The Manchester Guardian, May 7th
	1908. About twenty Waitresses at the Ceylon Café, Piccadilly, struck work in a dramatic fashion yesterday. It was between one and two o'clock, when business is usually very brisk, that they put aside their badges of service – white caps and aprons – and announced their intention of leaving the place as a protest against the treatment of a fellow servant."

THE WAITRESSES CHEER.

WAITRESS 1(CONT'D):	"A little later in the day the management drew from their staffs at other restaurants belonging to the Company, and peedily filled up the vacancies."
WAITRESS 3:	So that's it? We're all out on our ears?
WAITRESS 2:	I told you to let things be.

END OF SCENE.

CAXTON HALL, 1908:

THE WAITRESSES DRESS THE TABLE FOR A MEETING - PUT ON A CLOTH, A VASE OF FLOWERS, A GLASS OF WATER, PAPERS. OVER THIS

MARY: But I'd watched that café manager, strutting about like the cock of the yard. And I saw the other waitresses, good, hard working women bowed down by long hours, low pay and unfair treatment. And I knew the time had come. Working-class women, ordinary women like us everywhere were starting to unionise.

We went to a meeting of the Manchester and Salford Women's Trades Council at Caxton Hall, Salford.

MARY AND THE WAITRESSES TAKE UP POSITIONS AT THE TABLE, READY TO ADDRESS THE MEETING.

WAITRESS 1: The managing director says the conditions of employment are as good as could be desired.

MARY: On our feet for fourteen hours a day without a proper break –

WAITRESS 1: He told the newspaper that, with commission –

WAITRESS 2: – at six pence in every pound taken –

WAITRESS 3: – the waitresses are paid between fourteen and nineteen shillings a week.

MARY: He's a liar!

WAITRESS 1: Most I earned there was eleven shillings and four pence.

WAITRESS 3: Some weeks, I was lucky to come out with seven.

He says sick grants are made, provided a girl has proved herself efficient in her duties.

MARY: Women sacked for being ill-

WAITRESS 3: He says none of us has ever mplained of any grievance.

MARY: – and dismissed for raising legitimate concerns.

WAITRESS 1: This is not fair, or right, or just.

WAITRESSES: (TOGETHER)Support the waitresses!

MARY: And the meeting listened.

WAITRESS 1: A collection was taken on our behalf -

WAITRESS 3: – Four pounds and sixteen shillings to help tide us over until we could find employment.

WAITRESS 1: Conditions at the café improved.

WAITRESS 2: Though we didn't get our jobs back.

MARY: We needed to organise. Rules were drawn up and the Café Workers Union was formed.

(END OF SCENE)

THE WAITRESSES PREPARE FOR THE MARCH THEY HAND OUT SONGSHEETS, UNROLL THE BANNER, SET OUT PLACARDS. OVER THIS -

WAITRESS 1: Mary Quaile became assistant organiser, and later organising secretary, of Manchester and Salford Women's Trades Council. She was elected to the Approved Society

	of the General Federation of Trade Unions, a position she held for more than 25 years.
WAITRESS 2:	She campaigned for the enfranchisement of women. When the First World War broke out, she spoke out against the fighting, and was a member of the No Conscription Fellowship. At least one of her four brothers was conscripted and, when he was invalided out, she became his carer. She was active in the Manchester Relief Committee.
WAITRESS 1:	I'm on a zero hours contract: some weeks there's work, some weeks nothing.
WAITRESS 3:	In 1919, she became National Women's Organiser for the Dock, Wharf & Riverside Workers' Union, which later joined with the Transport & General Workers Union: she remained in post until 1933 when ill-health forced her to retire.
WAITRESS 2:	The restaurant is so busy some nights I don't even have time to go to the toilet.
WAITRESS 1:	1924, appointed to the General Council of the Trades Union Congress. Attended the National Conference of Labour Women.
WAITRESS 3:	I work hard but I often have to choose whether to buy food or pay the rent.
WAITRESS 2:	Mary was a member of the TUC Women Workers Group, and actively encouraged the organisation of women in trade unions.
WAITRESS 1:	I have to buy my own order pads and pens.
WAITRESS 3:	She went, in 1924, to the conference of International Women Trade Unionists in Vienna. She was chair of the 1925 women's trade union delegation to the Soviet Union, where she spent four months.
WAITRESS 2:	I was sacked for taking time off to look after my sick baby.
WAITRESS 1:	After being elected again in 1925 to the General Council, Mary became one of the most prominent women trade unionists in Britain.
WAITRESSES:	What about me/what about now?
	THE WAITRESSES REMOVE THEIR APRONS, **CAPS**.
MARY:	Sisters! Brothers! You have long suffered hardship and exploitation. Everyday, up and down this land – this wealthy land, built by the sweat and toil of your mothers and fathers – you and your fellow workers are subject to inequality and injustice. Poverty wages; long hours; dangerous and dirty working conditions; zero hours contracts. Dismissed without notice; threatened with the sack for speaking out against those abuses.
	You walk the streets, and you trawl the internet, looking for work, for the means to feed and house yourself and your families. And you are told you should be grateful for the wretched conditions you have been offered. No more!
	Just as there is dignity in work – as our government and

masters are fond of telling us, their justification for cutting and withholding welfare support - so workers demand to be treated with dignity and with respect.

Fair pay is not a gift: it is an entitlement. Equal pay is not a hope: it is a right. A contract – with set hours; holiday and sickness pay; proper breaks; clean and safe working conditions; proper training – this is your due, not some politician's mealy- mouthed aspiration for 'when economic conditions allow.

And your ability to withhold your labour is not a privilege to be snatched away at the whim of the ruling party: it is your birthright, won by generations of union men and women.

Join the union! Working together, we can achieve real progress. Together we can stand up to injustice. Together, we are strong.

WAITRESS 1:	In 1935 Mary was elected Vice-President of the Trades Council, the first woman officer of the Council. From 1936 to 1958 she acted as Treasurer.

In 1951 she was awarded the TUC Silver Badge for Trades Council Officers at a reception at Belle Vue attended by some four thousand people.

> WAITRESS 2 HANDS MARY THE TUC SILVER BADGE: THE WAITRESSES APPLAUD.

WAITRESS 3:	Mary Quaile died in 1958. Her obituary read; "her determination to get trade unionism for women accepted was often met with jeers, boos, rotten apples, and threats of violence.
WAITRESS 1:	"She spoke at hundreds of factory gate meetings in both the East End of London and Manchester; she never betrayed any sign of fear when faced with hostility.
WAITRESS 2:	"Her warmth and lovable personality won for her many friends in the labour and trade union movement."
MARY:	We'd best get this march underway then, hadn't we?

> THE WAITRESSES PICK UP THEIR PLACARDS AND SING "DARE TO BE FREE"

WAITRESSES & MARY: Women will you join us, As we march for liberty?
For there is strength in union, And that strength will set us free.
Alone, we have no power,
And we bear inequity.
Take my hand, and join the union
And together we'll be free.

Chorus:

There's a thread that links our stories;
It's that thread that makes us strong.
Sisters, stand beneath our banner,
Join your voices to our song.
Take my hand; we'll share the burden.
Take my hand, we'll stronger be,
As we fight against injustice.
Sisters, dare to be free.
Men, tell your wives and daughters

That the union is the way
To end abuse and tyranny,
Ensure all get better pay.
All we have's our sweat and toil;
All we have's our industry;
We'll withhold it in the struggle,
In the battle to be free.
Join your voices, all you women,
Let the bosses hear your song.
For together we are mighty;
For together we are strong.
If one hundred thousand women
March against adversity;
If we organize, my sisters,
Then women will be free!

MARY HANDS THE TUC SILVER BADGE TO WAITRESS 1.

MARY: There's still work to be done.

MARY AND THE WAITRESSES LEAD OUT THE MARCH,
SINGING.

Pictures from Dare To be Free

"Everybody should be in a union": an interview with NEU activist Trish Fay

by Bernadette Hyland

On Saturday 29th April 2017 the Mary Quaile Club launched the website of the Minutes of the Manchester and Salford Women's Trades Union Council 1895-1919 as part of Manchester Trades Council May Day Festival.

This event was the culmination of a year-long project to transcribe the handwritten Minutes of the Council and place them on a website for all to read and make use of. We canvassed support among trade unions around the country and individuals who responded generously, and we were therefore able to finance both the transcription of the Minutes and the creation of a website containing both the transcription and pictures of the original minutes.

The Minute Books are of national significance, providing fascinating detail on the early days of trade union organisation amongst women workers. We were given the two volumes (comprising 760 pages) by Mary Quaile's descendants in 2016 who made contact with us in the course of our research for our pamphlet: *"Dare To Be Free" women in trade unions: past and present*. It seems that Mary took the volumes with her when the Women's Trades Council dissolved in April 1919: fortunately both she and her family had kept them in very good condition.

Lisa Turnbull of the Durham Teaching Assistants Campaign switched on the website, thus making the

link between the working class women of the past and the current generation of women campaigners.

Women's lives have changed enormously since the days of the MSWTUC. It was started by a group of philanthropists including C P Scott, the editor of the *Manchester Guardian* and Julia Gaskell. Their aim was to support working class women - who were then largely excluded from male dominated trade unions - and encourage them to set up their own organisations to campaign for decent pay and conditions.

Unlike women in the nineteenth century the DTAs were a group of highly skilled, largely women workers, employed by the local Council. In the main they were members of Unison (one of the biggest trade unions in the country) and had contracts of employment.

But in 2015 their employer Durham Council proposed a cut of 23% to their wages, while Unison wanted them to agree to the cuts. Feeling betrayed by their union they set up their own campaigning group and took their fight to the country and social media.

Trish Fay was one of the Durham Teaching Assistants who refused to accept cuts to their pay and conditions by a Labour Council and a complicit trade union.

Her story reflects a trend of action by workers to move from trade unions that fail to represent them to organising separately and then finding new organisations that would treat them with equality and justice.

The campaign by the DTAs reflected the ongoing undermining of our public services - services that employ many women - and the way in which important, largely female groups of workers have been thrown under the bus by organisations that were supposed to represent and defend their jobs and conditions.

In their fight with the Labour Council the women created their own organisation - CDTAAC (County Durham Teaching Assistants Action Committee) - and used every method possible, including social media, to shout out about the undermining of their profession and trashing of their pay and conditions.

Seven years on Trish, who became a union activist through the strike, is as fervent as ever about the importance of trade unions to improve and protect peoples' lives, both at work and outside.

Trish was born in the north east; her father was a shipyard worker. When the shipyards closed down he became a prison officer. The family then moved down to Wakefield and at the age of 15 Trish had to leave her friends and move to a new town – one where she would marry and have two children.

Trish has been a Teaching Assistant since 1986. In Wakefield she worked in a girls private school and after her marriage broke down she moved back to the north-east in 2008. She went into the state primary sector where she worked with some of the most challenging children.

When she qualified as a Nursery Nurses she had to do the Nursery Nursing Examination Board qualification. "You had to do exams and it was very different to the 12 week online courses that people are doing today."

Moving from the private educational sector to the state sector was a challenge for Trish. "It was a baptism of fire with many children who had special educational needs". She had never been in a union before, but when she joined the public sector there was one and she knew her late father would have encouraged her.

Most teaching assistants are women who work with children and, like many other groups of women

workers – such as care workers, cleaners and catering staff – they often face managements who label their work as women's work that is not skilled or valued. In 2015 she was one of the 2,700 Durham Teaching Assistant's who were now told that their jobs were to be downgraded.

"We were called to a meeting with our Head and told that we could not tell the parents what was happening and that if we did anything (at that time two TAs had started a Facebook page) there would be repercussions."

But the CDTAAC ignored this. They attended a meeting with their union, Unison at which over 300 people took part. "They just said 'you cannot do anything about it,' but our response was the opposite; 'we have got to do something.'"

The other union that represented the DTAs was the GMB. "They agreed the cuts without even consulting their members," says Trish.

The women got on with the job of defending their pay and conditions; publicising what was happening to them; and organising meetings with other TAs across the county. They made their own banner and produced badges and tee-shirts. Being a TA means you are adept at making things as cheaply as possible so their first banner was made with broomsticks from Home Bargains! They also took part in the Durham Miners Gala.

Social media played a major role in getting their message out to other TAs as well as other workers, both locally and across the country. "I taught myself to use social media including Twitter. In fact I became known as the Twitter mistress!" laughs Trish.

Faced with a hostile employer and a complicit union they took their campaign nationwide. A breakthough was an article on the dispute by *Guardian* journalist Aditya Chakrabortty, based on interviews with the TAs - "Treated like dirt, these teaching assistants have become the lions of Durham" - which was published on 6th September 2016: He wrote:

The TAs have been forced to fight for themselves. While they may not be militant, they do of course have decades of experience in organising and making something out of nothing. So they hold meetings, at which outside sympathisers expect a few handfuls to turn up. The women pack the halls full.

They mount demos outside the council offices, and what should be dull, sparsely attended affairs turn into something more like a sports

Trish as Twitter Mistress

day, with hundreds of women dancing about. They post songs on Youtube, produce merchandise, collect testimonies from members, and email assistants across the county. In short, they are doing what their union should be doing.

Chakrabortty compared the DTAs to the Grunwick strikers of 1976 – another largely women's strike, this time by Asian workers in the private sector - but both groups of workers were betrayed and sold out by their unions. The publicity from the article filled their campaign fund which went from £2,000 to £22,000

For over twenty months the women marched, demonstrated, spoke at meetings up and down the country and went on strike. And although the left-wing socialist Jeremy Corbyn was elected the leader of the Labour Party in September 2015 it made no difference to the local Labour Council which carried on with their cuts to the pay and conditions of the TAS.

As for Trish, she had had enough of the behaviour of Unison so she left and joined the Association of Teachers and Lecturers (ATL). However this union was not recognised by the Durham Council as representing TAs; they only recognised Unison and GMB.

In 2017 a ballot was held on an improved, but controversial deal, a deal that divided the TAS. On a turnout of 57%; 62% voted to accept. The GMB TA's were not balloted as they accepted earlier offers. Only the TAs in ATL voted to reject, 56% to 44% on a 60% turnout.

Trish feels bitter about the way the ballot was conducted; "No outsiders were allowed into the count – there were no observers". She also feels that the promises made about the deal were not

realised. "TAs lost money – from hundreds to thousands. Our contract has gone from 32 and a half hours to 37 with no extra money."

In September 2017 ATL became part of the new teaching union, the National Education Union (NEU) which would now recruit all staff who work in schools. In her school Trish represents 28 members who are all in the NEU, including some teachers.

Trish attends branch and district NEU meetings and support staff conferences. She says: "It is the NEU who are now paying for professional development training for staff as the schools cannot afford it." She was nominated as Representative of the Year for the Northern region – and given an award. The NEU have support staff on their National Executive and she is now the National representative on this body.

Trish says that the challenges of the Covid crisis showed the importance of the NEU to the school sector. "With little guidance and support from the government it was the NEU who stepped up and provided information on dealing with Covid and we shared it with all staff – not just our members. Even the Head Teacher was grateful for the information." She praises the union. "The NEU were brilliant in supporting staff and keeping the children and the staff safe."

In January 2021 an astonishing 400,000 members logged onto the NEU's Zoom call. NEU joint general secretary Kevin Courtney tweeted: "NEU on Zoom this morning. Figures in: 100k watched the whole meeting; 400k watched at least part of it. Is this the biggest meeting in UK political history?"

The previous weekend the union had recruited 6,000 new members after advising teachers that it was unsafe to return to school. The NEU also wrote to all employers, head teachers and principals offering them the same advice and encouraging them to move to remote learning instead.

The use of Zoom has opened up new ways for unions to reach members – and for members to reach their union. Trish says: "More people attend on Zoom than ever before and that goes for district and branch meetings."

After Covid the union intends to continue with a mixture of Zoom and face-to-face - including at the national conference - so as to encourage those who may still be shielding or have caring responsibilities to participate.

Trish's district in County Durham has a whole network on Whatsapp groups, not just for

Trish with Durham Teaching Assistants banner

representatives but also for different group e.g. LGBTQ. During Lockdown social meetings were held, including quiz nights.

This democratic working has continued post-Lockdown as Trish comments. "We are sharing information and guidance and there are now a lot more Health and Safety Officers and Covid representatives in the schools."

A big problem for Trish and support staff is that the local authority still refuses to recognise NEU as representing support staff. "We cannot actively recruit support staff and cannot take part in negotiations, although some local authorities do allow the NEU to take part. We should have recognition." She feels that this is still the case that the recognised trade unions, Unison and GMB, are "in the back pockets of the local authority."

Through her activity Trish has seen the good and bad side of trade union organisation. But she is still convinced that "everybody should be in a union. It is for your own protection - in the classroom, in your employment contract, over personal issues." Trish is heartened by the numbers of young people joining and being active in the union. "I came to activity later in life so it is good to see so many young people joining a union."

The website of the Manchester and Salford Women's Trades Council can be found here www.mswtuc.co.uk/

The website of the National Education Union can be found here https://neu.org.uk/

"We shouldn't have to be men and behave as men in order to be taken seriously in the world" A conversation between Katy Worley and Naomi Bridges from the feminist group *Make More Noise!*

Naomi: So I think it's safe to say Twitter has been a massive part of us coming together and our activism. I find it to be a real double edged sword; I've met so many amazing women but social media can be addictive and this sort of platform can really reward a certain type of jingoistic engagement. Likes, clicks, big dramatic statements.

Katy: Obviously the internet has been a great tool for feminists, especially in the pushback to the recent encroachment on women's rights. It's been essential to a lot of consciousness raising that's not happening in people's living rooms anymore. Well it is, on forums like *Mumsnet* which you access from your living room. But there is a limit to this kind of engagement that can lead to a cult of personality, a cruelty. When you're face to face with a woman you wouldn't say the things you say online. There's a censorship too, men who post rape and death threats are fine, but if you say a man is a man that's not allowed.

As feminists we're beholden to speaking palatably to men and male power structures, run by men on Facebook, and if we come afoul of them we're removed. It allows men to shape the discourse. Some of the best voices in this movement are removed and the voices that are left have to speak a certain way and moderate their language. It has a chilling effect.

Naomi: Yes *Make More Noise*, and your personal account, have had multiple twitter bans. Often it's been for speaking the truth and pointing out male violence. We've used blunt language but even if we're speaking plainly it doesn't stop what we're saying being the truth.

I'd been a feminist for a while but had taken a step back in recent years, I felt unconnected with mainstream feminism but it was social media that ignited my activism again. I had no idea about the proposed Gender Recognition Act (GRA) reforms until I saw it online and I think I started engaging with stuff on Twitter before I made it to a real life meeting, but I only found out about the meeting through Twitter. I remember getting to the first meeting I went to and breathing a sigh of relief. A few months later it was another similar meeting where you and I were both attended, but I don't think we actually ended up chatting that much at the time?

Katy: I remember being in two minds about whether I would even go to the event. I didn't know anyone who was going, I just knew a couple of my Twitter pals had said they would go. I very nearly didn't go, I was that scared. I went there and it was like "wow, I can say what I like, I am with my tribe." Yeah, I didn't meet you then.

When you're born a tomboy, you're always going to end up some kind of feminist. You can see how you're excluded from fun and high status activities. I grew up in the era of girl power and ladette culture, I was a bit of a ladette, trying to beat men at their own game. I always identified as a feminist and thought it was something every woman should be. As time went on I realised trying to out-men men wasn't going to work and there is a lack of appreciation of the differences, which you learn in the gender critical thing. It's been great for me to embrace my womanhood - whatever that means - and to realise it's okay for women to be different. We don't have to be men. We shouldn't have to be men and behave as men in order to be taken seriously in the world.

Naomi: Yeah I felt really connected by attending those meetings. Connected to women, connected to the movement, and connected to my own womanhood in my own way. After that meeting a few of us ended up in a Twitter chat group and invigorated we decided to do a bit of direct action! It was pretty nerve wracking but we had a laugh. I remember thinking, because you were the only one who turned up, "oh, she actually turns up to stuff and wants to get stuff done."

Katy: The week before we met was interesting. We were all really interested in doing activism. We knew we were all local women and we just wanted to just do something - anything. I met you at a bar in the gay village and it was almost like a blind date - like, "hello fellow feminist."

I didn't expect to have the impact I did with a few stickers. I think a lot of women are finding this - an inroad into activism through stickering. For some reason they seem to really trigger people. I think it's great! A gateway drug into activism!

Naomi: Yeah I remember searching for you in that bar and as soon as I sat down you joked about wearing all black to be incognito. After that I think we

MAKE MORE NOISE!

1 WOMEN ARE OPPRESSED BECAUSE OF THEIR BODIES (I.E SEX) AND THEIR ABILITY TO CREATE NEW LIFE.

2 GENDER IS A SOCIAL CONSTRUCT WHICH MAKES WOMEN'S INFERIORITY TO MEN SEEM NATURAL. IT MUST BE ABOLISHED.

3 THERE IS A COVERT, GLOBAL TREND TO REPLACE SEX WITH GENDER IN LAW. THIS WE MUST RESIST.

4 WOMEN'S LABOUR WITHIN THE FAMILY IS INVISIBLE. MOTHERS AND DAUGHTERS DESERVE MORE.

5 PORN IS ANTI-WOMAN PROPAGANDA THAT IS NORMALISING RAPE AND WOMEN'S SUBJUGATION UNDER MEN.

6 SEX WORK IS NOT WORK. IT EXPLOITS WOMEN AND DRIVES A GLOBAL NETWORK OF SEX SLAVERY. WOMEN'S BODIES ARE NOT FOR SALE. EVER.

7 YOU CAN'T BUY EMANCIPATION. LIBERATION IS NOT A BRAND OF LIPSTICK.

8 MAINSTREAM FEMINISM HAS ABANDONED WOMEN AND SERVES ONLY THE NEEDS OF RICH WOMEN AND ALL MEN.

9 RIGHT WING MEN AND LEFT WING MEN HATE WOMEN EQUALLY. WOMEN SHOULD STOP PROVIDING THEM WITH THEIR POLITICAL LABOUR.

10 NICE WOMEN DON'T MAKE HISTORY. FIGHT BACK NOW MAKE MORE NOISE!

realised that we were two women who wanted to Get Stuff Done. We started *Make More Noise* as an idea for a collective that could speak to every day women who weren't necessarily knee deep in feminism or activism. We launched with a blog post and you wrote the first blog article, it was great and got loads of views. I remember thinking - there is clearly a niche for this. Women want this sort of content. It's not all focused around the GRA, we care about other issues. But the GRA and related issues is a big one and was taking up so much oxygen at the time.

Katy: I remember we decided to launch before that article, and it was the Sunday night and I saw the Lily Madigan thing unfolding. I thought "this will be great if I screenshot the narrative" and put it out there quickly. There are so many bubbles and storms in teacups in the movement. I think a lot have been lost to time because we hadn't been so quick to get them down on paper.

Naomi: Yeah and they give a really good snapshot, like a microcosm into what we're banging on about and the dynamics at play

Katy: Yeah, the Lily Madigan thing was great because it gets to the heart of what is happening in youth politics. The next day I contacted the people involved and I was surprised how much they wanted to talk. It made it seem a bit more journalistic, I was

MAKE MORE NOISE!

chatting to the people directly and not just writing up a blog with my own opinion.

I was shocked by the number of views, 10k or something? It inspired me. I don't think we've ever written an article as popular as that one. It just goes to show what can be done today, with social media. It was so easy to find and talk to people. It shows how anyone can become a citizen journalist.

Naomi: Yeah we wrote up a couple of other events and direct actions. The one at 5-clouds was quite fun as it was organised so quickly and then we wrote it up. And yeah, if we hadn't then the details might just have been lost to time.

Whose idea was it for the podcast? You came up with the name for it, *Suffragette City Radio* as well as the name *Make More Noise*. You've always been great at this sort of thing. I had the tech and the skills to put it together. I think we really complemented each other. We've covered some great content on it, as well as some nonsense when you and I go off on a rant. But your story about your meeting with Angela Rayner has a LOT of listens

Katy: The Helen Steel one too. It's a great interview and a great topic. The spy cops thing is horrifying really, and then being cut out for her gender critical position. One thing the trans stuff has shown us is the misogyny on the left. Helen Steel was being spied on by the authorities. In such an intimate way, an intimate betrayal. At the same time her so-called comrades don't respect women.

Naomi: I'm reminded of the SWP rape accusations. Leftist groups aren't always an ally to women.

Katy: It's the same kind of misogyny. It shows the way cops could operate because the movement doesn't respect women. Here's a woman who has done so much in the movement, it's a small movement and she knows these people, but just to see how quickly and violently she was ejected

because she didn't toe the line on the trans stuff.

When we started off the podcast we weren't really friends at the time but throughout making it we became friends which is lovely. We have a nice rapport and it's quite natural.

Naomi: Yeah, the first episode is a bit awkward! We didn't really know each other! We really got into a groove though.

We then decided to expand and put on an event, it was hard work and a lot of hard graft. Nobody ever tells you about the drudgery of activism do they? The emails, the logs, the checking venue availability. Again, I think social media really helped launched us and keep us connected to lots of women. Our multiple Twitter bans not withstanding...

Katy: I think the decision to do the event was something we discussed but we decided to do it after yet again another Twitter ban. We wanted to create a space for in real life discussions because whilst it's great to be on Twitter you can't really form the connections.

Naomi: That's how we met.

Katy: Yeah, creating events where women can meet is as important as the actual event itself. It's important for women to come along to these things and meet like minded people because it can be quite isolating to be gender critical when the rest of your community have been drinking the Kool-aid.

Naomi: Even during lockdown we tried to put out a podcast and keep something going. The 4th wave really has so much to thank technology for. We also made a decision to criticise the corona response from a feminist perspective, which didn't win us a lot of friends. The GRA issue is a hot rod but this felt like something else. I'm really glad we had each other during that.

Katy: At times it felt like we were going mad, and having you was good. Having a group of women who could see things the way they were. We'd been isolated by taking this gender critical position and then this came along - we were isolated within being isolated! I'm quite confused as to how far people could think, and it didn't seem very far. Women have got their hands full with trying to fight back against gender ideology and other issues, I don't expect women to prioritise all the things I do, we have all these battles. But it was frustrating, all our civil liberties were stripped away and contingent on compliance. In service to the pharmaceutical industry who are the ones making a profit from transitioning children. And they were actively hostile to us as well.

Naomi: Yeah it was hard. I didn't expect everyone to agree completely with us but I wanted to have that discussion, which is what we've always been about, having discussions and asking questions.

So are we the 4th wave? What even is the 4th wave? I think I read somewhere that some people are pinning it as starting around maybe 2012 when a lot of feminist thinkers and bloggers started getting traction on social media and a lot of young women became interested and older women who hadn't previously considered themselves feminists were on Facebook and the like and wanted to get involved. I suppose we are but do people in the wave ever acknowledge that they are in the wave? What are the good things and bad things about the 4th wave?

Katy: Good is the internet. It's the opportunities and challenges that come with the internet age. On one hand it's great to connect with like-minded people. On the other you see the tendency for group think and a tribal us vs them approach. And let's not forget the Men's Right's Activists of all stripes are also meeting and communicating on these platforms. And they seem to have the support of Silicon Valley giants. They let rape and death threats against women stand and mean while women who quote the law or statistics can get their accounts removed. A big problem is tech censorship and the bounds of what we're allowed to say being dictated by a small group of white men in California.

Naomi: Yeah it's horrifying. Being a feminist and being critical of gender ideology, the corona response, and other sacred cows has made me much more of an advocate for Free Speech. Do we think we've contributed in our way to the 4th wave?

Katy: I think so, I think the events were really important. They were spaces where women could connect. All I ever wanted to do was encourage other people into activism. When I saw how much you and I got done with two of us, it was great. In Manchester

Naomi and Katy at a *Make More Noise!* event

we did three events in one year, it created a bit of buzz about the city.

Naomi: Important events as well, we tackled hot topics like domestic violence, detransition and hate crimes. I was especially proud of the detransition one. It felt important.

Katy: I think it was the first, and we had great access. People like David Bell who has become a bit of a public figure on this, and Keira Bell spoke there.

It was a *Make More Noise* event that inspired Posie Parker's Speakers Corner events. I like to think of ripples in a pond, just because you aren't credited with something doesn't mean we've not influenced people or helped to create things. We certainly seem to have ruffled a few feathers! If people are trying to silence you, you must be doing something right.

Naomi: What do we see as the future of this movement? Feminism more broadly and the gender ideology movement? I do believe we've gotten through the worst but it is by no means over. There is a lot of legislation by the back door and a lot of institutions and corporations keep pushing through nonsense policies! I think that ultimately it won't disappear but will be considered a fringe movement with loud voices, but hopefully a much smaller influence. I'm also worried about the general encroachment on civil liberties. For feminists and everyone else.

Katy: I think all worlds lead to porn as far as I'm concerned! Porn is creating young autogynephiles. Young girls being raised in a porn saturated society, young lesbians seeing their sexuality as a porn category. I think there's something behind porn that leads to civil liberties like you say. Feminists have analysis of porn objectifying and dehumanising women, but it does it on a general level too. It encourages and is linked to the dehumanising process where people are quick to exclude others from society. There's a real ease with which people can be othered. There's a viciousness with which you can exclude people.

Naomi: Yeah, porn is really violent and getting more and more extreme. Right in the palm of the hand of every 10 year old.

Katy: You basically have an entire generation of children who have been groomed by porn, we still don't know how that is going to play out and affect society. I think the battles for feminism going forward will be surrogacy, sex industry, paedophilia being legalised.

Naomi: I'm so glad I met you, in the face of all this bleakness we put something in the world.

Katy: It does sound bleak doesn't it? But what's great is women have risen to the challenge and women realising they had skills they didn't know they had. The connections that have been formed will last a long time. If gender ideology ended tomorrow many women would still be fighting for women's rights. Relationships have formed, and we're definitely a friendship/partnership.

There's a Pankhurst quote that goes along the lines of "if you piss off women they won't stop."

Naomi: Hang on, let me Google it. "Women are very slow to rouse, but once they are aroused, once they are determined, nothing on earth and nothing in heaven will make women give way; it is impossible."

Katy: Yeah that'll do.

Make More Noise can be found at https://makemorenoisemanc.wixsite.com/mysite

Statue of Mrs Pankhurst, Manchester